Islam
and
the Living Law

ISLAM AND THE LIVING LAW

THE IBN AL-ARABI APPROACH

Eric Winkel

Karachi
Oxford University Press
Oxford New York Delhi
1997

Oxford University Press, Walton Street, Oxford OX2 6DP
Oxford New York
Athens Auckland Bangkok Bombay
Calcutta Cape Town Dar es Salaam Delhi
Florence Hong Kong Istanbul Karachi
Kuala Lumpur Madras Madrid Melbourne
Mexico City Nairobi Paris Singapore
Taipei Tokyo Toronto
and associated companies in
Berlin Ibadan

Oxford is a trade mark of Oxford University Press

ISBN 0 19 577690 9

Printed in Pakistan at
S. M. Printers Karachi
Published by
Ameena Saiyid, Oxford University Press
5-Bangalore Town, Sharae Faisal
P.O. Box 13033, Karachi-75350, Pakistan.

Contents

Preface vii

Notes to Preface xi

Chapter 1 : Politics, State, and Islam 1

I. The *Fiqh* in the Political Realm 4
II. Caliphal Politics 6
III. The *Fiqh* 9

Notes to Chapter 1 11

Chapter 2 : Spirituality and the *Fiqh* 15

I. The Khawarij, Batiniyyah, and Ibahiyyah Types 16

Notes to Chapter 2 25

Chapter 3 : Ibn al-Arabi and *Ijtihad* 28

I. *Fiqh* and *Qada* 35
II. Naming 37
III. Logic and Analogy 41

Notes to Chapter 3 45

Chapter 4 : Ibn al-Arabi's Legal Literalism 51

I. First Case 54
II. Second Case 57

Notes to Chapter 4 62

Chapter 5 : The Polysemantic Quran 65

I. Recitations 67
II. Authorities 67
III. Arguments 70
IV. Ibn al-Arabi's Position 78

Notes to Chapter 5 83

Chapter 6 : Three Passages 86

I. The First Passage 86
II. The Second Passage 90
III. The Third Passage 94

Notes to Chapter 6 97

Afterword 99
Notes to Afterword 103
Index of Quranic Quotations 104
Index of Hadith Quotations 108
Index 113

Preface

The entire question of power, violence, and politics started intriguing me when I tried to locate power in the Islamic world-view, during the time I was writing my dissertation. Soon after, I began to take up the challenges of Foucault and Habermas and to study the whole idea of power, authority, and discourse in a Muslim context. For a while, I had thought that the relationship of deconstruction to the kinds of radical hermeneutics found in saints, from Meister Eckhardt to Ibn al-Arabi, would be promising. There is a certain initial, formal interrelation between what Sufis do to deconstruct texts, and what the post-modernists and post-structuralists are doing. This interrelationship is somewhat superficial and I have since dropped the entire enterprise, convinced of the sufficiency of classical discourses developed in Islam. As will become clear, I do not simply have an academic interest in these questions, hence the engaged style of my writing.

One of those promising indigenous discourses is called *fiqh*. The word *fiqh* conventionally means the set of rigid rules and regulations formulated by generations of overly legalistic minds. True, such a *fiqh* could never interest anyone with an iota of spirituality and intelligence; however, the word could be restored to its original meaning which is based on the Quranic phrase *So they may understand the din* (religion) [9:122], where 'understand' is *tafaqquh*.[1] I also like the phrase *tafaqquh ruhani*, which could be defined as spiritual-legal discourse. The word 'sapiential', wisdom perspectives, used by Sachiko Murata in *The Tao of Islam* points to the same concept. Sachiko Murata contrasts in that excellent book the conventional understanding of *fiqh* and shariah with the sapiential (knowledge). But rather than turn over the definition of shariah to the fundamentalists and the anti-sapiential types, I suggest we rediscover wisdom in the spiritual-legal discourse.

This is not to say that one can pick up any of the classical works and find unmitigated wisdom throughout. It was not until I had studied Ibn al-Arabi that I began to appreciate the classical works of scholars like Ibn Qudamah, Ibn Hajar, and al-Nawawi. Not surprisingly, classical scholars are immersed in their cultures and world-views. It takes a sympathetic reader to allow a classical writer the occasional diatribe; I can even accept that in some cultural systems women are intellectually inferior, a child's single act of disobedience is the precursor of total societal chaos, and men and women are forced to know each other only from physical and emotional distances in highly constrained and charged arenas. Ibn al-Arabi's works are in sharp contrast. What I have concluded so far is that Ibn al-Arabi's works are not about him or his ideas, which would make him as culturally anchored as Ibn Qudamah or Ibn Hajar. His works show processes, open windows, reflect on language and reflection, and help prepare the listener of sacred text. He is universal because, while reading his works, our eyes follow his finger pointing to the universal and his finger ceases to exist.

Ibn al-Arabi is the mystic scholar of the thirteenth century whom contemporary Muslims, including most of the scholars, associate with dangerous, gnostic intentions. What Ibn al-Arabi is, is the most direct, authentic, and literal purveyor of the divine messages entrusted to messengers and prophets upon insight. What I try to do here is take up once again the discussion of spiritual-legal *fiqh* which Ibn al Arabi put in articulate form seven hundred years ago.

This discussion is alive in parts of the Sunni world, even though the vast majority of Sunnis, if they have heard the name, think they despise Ibn al-Arabi. What has happened is that Ibn al-Arabi's style and insights have been passed down through the ages. One can find in a tiny mosque in the middle of nowhere, an old man who has some strange interpretations of a verse of the Quran, interpretations which are accurate and which come from Ibn al-Arabi's tradition—even though the old man will tell you, and may believe it himself, that Ibn al-Arabi is a heretic.

In the Shi'ite world, Ibn al-Arabi is well-known and studied, but what happens, in my view, is that Ibn al-Arabi himself is not studied: his disciples are studied. His disciples wanted to transform—and succeeded in transforming to a philosopher's satisfaction—the master's insights into a formal philosophical system. This philosophical system is characterized by a phrase which Ibn al-Arabi himself never used: *wahdat al-wujud*, the Unity of Existence. Invariably, Muslim intellectuals will identify Ibn al-Arabi as a philosopher, or more precisely, a pantheistic philosopher of *wahdat al-wujud*.

Ibn al-Arabi is misunderstood because his use of language refuses stability and reification. He uses various language formats in order to avoid being constrained. So one quickly learns to avoid pigeon-holing him. Some examples: as we saw, the phrase most associated with Ibn al-

Arabi was never used by him; the Sunnis take his insights but denigrate his name; his disciples create a full-blown system out of insights which are themselves defiantly anti-systematic; the Shi'ites base an entire philosophy on that system; modern Sufis think he is dangerous, but the only danger to them is that Ibn al-Arabi would tell some of them to forget their guru and practice the shariah; orientalists were interested in him because he seemed to be anti-shariah, but reviving his insights would actually serve to invigorate and validate the shariah. In short, everything one thinks about Ibn al-Arabi must be revised. Ibn al-Arabi forces you to realize that everything you think you know about Islam must be radically challenged and revised in light of the Quran and Sunna.

What this book does, then, is take up this technique again. This work was completed during a Fulbright Scholarship. I do not take a very 'historical' view, as I have been engaged in circulating among Muslim scholars in the realm of ideas. I have been concerned with 'Islamic ideology', Islamization, and in the many ways of understanding contemporary political situations intellectually, from the US to Malaysia to Pakistan and many places in between.

I am interested primarily in power and politics in Islam—in the Islam of a more direct, immediate, and insightful group of Muslims called the ulema, those ulema who know Allah, for that is the root of the word. And their most articulate and prolific associate is Ibn al-Arabi.

The spiritual-legal discourse of Ibn al-Arabi (and Sufi scholars in general) centres on *hukm*: Muslim religious life is the effort to follow the *hukm* of Allah and His messenger, where *hukm* can be described as the determinative property of things. What is right and what is wrong, what is good and bad, appropriate and inappropriate is determined by the *hukm* of Allah and His messenger. When and how it is appropriate to pray, give charity, fast, or make the pilgrimage is the concern of the spiritual-legal discourse (the *fiqh*).

Given that there is a creator and guidance, and messengers who deliver guidance, the spiritual-legal discourse focuses on realizing guidance in changing contexts. Since Allah used human language (in this case, Quranic Arabic) and human messengers (in this case, Muhammad) to convey guidance, the focus of *fiqh* is human language, history, and context. Each novel situation will present the spiritual-legal practitioner with choices, and choosing the right, good, and appropriate behaviour will depend on matching the articulated guidance of revelation (including normative prophetic practice) with the unique situation. The one who is good at this matching process, good at determining the *hukm* (h.k.m.) of the situation, may be called the *hakim* (h.k.m.), two words which share the same root.

To be human is to be immersed in ambiguity. The sapiential tradition, the spiritual-legal discourse, embraces that ambiguity and seeks articulate assessments of appropriate behaviour centred on identifying the *hukm* of any moment. The technical side of this process is conventionally called the *fiqh*, but the word *fiqh* classically carried the original sense of 'understanding the religion'. For example, the verse (5:6) in the Quran which establishes the means to become purified for prayer (*salah*) is polysemantic, as we shall see, and may be read as saying that the feet be washed, wiped, washed *or* wiped, or washed *and* wiped. How to determine the appropriate action is the subject of *fiqh* and includes debates about linguistics and about the relationship of the Quran to prophetic practice (Sunna).

What Ibn al-Arabi does in the section on the mysteries of the pillars of Islam found in his massive *Futuhat al-Makkiyyah*, is to recover this original, humanistic perspective of divine guidance.[2] Where fundamentalism silences ambiguity (and thereby silences the divine), Ibn al-Arabi works with the fullness of language and context and with the human situation. This work is an effort to apply that humanistic perspective to divine guidance.

Notes

1. Arabic words usually have three letter roots, and so *fiqh, faqih* (one who does *fiqh*) and *tafaqquh* (to *fiqh* something) can all be classified by the radical letters f.q.h.

   About the word *fiqh*, Ibn Manzur (d. 711 A. H./1311 C. E.) says, '*Fiqh* is knowledge of something and understanding something'. And others say, '*fiqh* in its root is understanding'. Allah said, *So they would tafaqqahu the din*, that is, so that they would be knowers (ulema) of it and teach the *fiqh* of Allah; and the Prophet prayed for Ibn Abbas' sake, '*Allahumma*, teach him the *din* and teach him the *fiqh* of interpretation', that is, teach him the *fiqh* of interpretation and its meanings. Allah answered his prayer, and Ibn Abbas became one of the most knowledgeable of the people of his time of the Book of Allah.
2. See my *Mysteries of Purity: Ibn al-Arabi's asrar al-taharah*, 1995 (Cross Cultural Publications, Box 506, Notre Dame, Indiana 46556).

CHAPTER 1

Politics, State, and Islam

The ulema over the centuries have developed a structure for determining the entire set of rules and regulations arising from the Quran and the Sunna (normative practice) of His messenger, Muhammad (*sallaLlahu alayhi wa sallam*).[1] This structure is called *fiqh* and is a legal discourse. But this legal discourse has been marginalized and attacked from many quarters, and for that reason few people are aware of the political ideas which the ulema hold. This chapter attempts to convey certain traditionally held political ideas of the ulema which will challenge conventional political notions held by some political scientists and students of Islamic civilization.

The ulema and the Islamic legal discourse (*fiqh*) have been continually and ferociously attacked, even from within the Muslim world, from many quarters—from secularists to modernists, reformists to fundamentalists. If these groups have one thing in common, it is a desire for power, and more specifically for state-centred schemes for Muslim progress.

Simply stated, the ulema stand in their way as modern state centralization has historically been shunned by the ulema.[2] In fact, the very essence of the ulema project—that edifice erected to determine rules and regulations from the revelation—is its decentralization, slow accumulation of positions and argumentation, local dominion, and diffusion. No one person can define and represent the Islamic experience, so the ulema resist Islam being centralized in the person of the nation-state leader, or in any university or institute. And as for state-centred schemes for progress, in accord with traditional religions, the ulema do not see progress as a virtue. As Norbert Wiener remarks,

> Most of us are too close to the idea of progress to take cognizance either of the fact that this belief belongs only to a small part of recorded history, or of

> the other fact, that it represents a sharp break with our own religious professions and traditions.[3]

The importance of the nation-state and the concept of progress to the dominant voice of politics in and about the Muslim world, helps explain why the ulema are portrayed as the enemy or at least as the obstacle, to necessary 'change' and 'development'. But they are not unique in this respect.

Jerry Mander[4] in his book *In the Absence of the Sacred*, quotes Oren Lyons, describing legal procedures of the Iroquois Nation: 'We meet and just keep talking until there's nothing left but the obvious truth, and both (disputing) families agree on the solution'.[5] I was struck by the similarity between this description and that of Lawrence Rosen of a *qadi* (judge) in a Moroccan town:

> For rather than being aimed simply at the invocation of state or religious power, rather than being devoted mainly to the creation of a logically consistent body of legal doctrine, the aim of the *qadi* is to put people back in the position of being able to negotiate their own permissible relationships without predetermining just what the outcome of those negotiations ought to be.[6]

What the ulema share with other traditional knowledge-elites is a desire to preserve a social realm where law is played out in the communal arena with language (or other discursive formats), where not only contention is resolved, but also societal definition and direction is nurtured. This definition and direction comes from the community itself, and not from a media dominated by huge corporations or the government, or from a priestly class of lawyers who design and prosecute laws. In fact, there seems to be no place in their vision for the totalitarian, corporate, legal fiction called the State which we take for granted.

The word *qadi* recalls the Arabic word's meaning of one who settles the affair (*qada*), and Rosen shows how the discretion given to the *qadi*—a discretion typically criticized by Western observers as laxity—allows him to make law a 'metasystem which creates order in a universe that is often experienced in a more disorderly way'.[7] The disputants are facilitated by the *qadi* to continue defining the situation until the solution is obvious to all. Consensus developed over time and not coercion, is the central product of this legal activity.

There is a great chasm between a 'traditional' society, which will mean here a society which organizes itself around divine guidance,[8] and a 'modern' society, which means a society with a state. As we shall see, the concept of state which has fully emerged in the last hundred years or so, and which saturates our field of vision, is alien to many traditional societies and to central activities of Islamic civilization. Yet when we want to investigate politics in Islam, we tend to look for states and at monarchical rulers like caliphs, sultans, and amirs; and when fundamentalists dream, they dream of a powerful, Utopian Islamic State. The fact remains that politics in Islamic civilization is located predominately in quite a different arena, and the ulema, including Ibn Taymiyyah, traditionally resisted all kinds of forces which might have potentially led to the kind of state powers which we have seen recently.

The dream of an Islamic State seems to include visions of sticks taken to rebellious Muslims, timorous non-Muslims citizens, and autocratic rulers on white horses solving all the prevailing problems. But the preoccupation with caliphate seems entirely modern, arising especially in the face of the humiliation suffered at the hands of nineteenth and twentieth century imperialist powers. Historically, Muslim communities throughout the world established the shariah by themselves, not *ex cathedra*, as the central focus of their community. Glimpses into daily life, chosen from hagiographic accounts of Sufis and their travels, popular poetry, inscriptions, and accounts of peasant revolts, reveal Muslim communities implementing the shariah themselves, striving thereby for a just society. In fact, the very word government (*hukumah*) in Arabic,[9] as recorded by the lexicographer Ibn Manzur below conveys a negative role for government, not a positive one.

> The Arab says *hakam-tu,* I prevented someone and *hakam-tu,* I averted someone with the meaning of I prevented someone and I averted someone. In this category, one says about the *hakim* among people that he is *hakim* because he prevents the oppressor from oppression. Al-Mundhiri reported from Abu Talib that he said about their statement *hakama* Allah among us, that al-Asma'i said the root of *hukumah* [government] is averting the oppressor from oppression.[10]

Here the government's role is simply to prevent oppression, because positive political benefits arise directly from practising the shariah. There is no place in this Arab conception of *hukumah* for massive bureaucracies, governmental spending and taxing, standing armies and governments. This conception suggests that government is quite an incidental affair, necessary only to stop the oppressor, and that the real political activity of the community is to be found elsewhere—and I suggest that place is the communal arena of the *fiqh*.

I. The *Fiqh* in the Political Realm

In this chapter, I want to refocus the way we look at politics in Islam, locating 'the political' in the contemporary legal discourses (here the *fiqh*) in operation in many Muslim communities for a thousand or more years. Two consequences especially arise from this refocusing: first, we shall discover a massive amount of information about politics in historical Muslim communities; second, we shall rediscover a means to engage in a discourse which is not alleged to be transparent (with hidden agendas and machinations), but which is contestable at every stage of the argument, open to a great diversity of participants, and is true to its roots in the revealed data.

The ulema traditionally exercised a distancing from encroaching state power. Indeed, we find great animosity among the ulema, including fundamentalist favourites like Ibn Taymiyyah, for emerging state power.[11] According to Rosen, the law 'provides a context for the peaceable formation by individuals of their own ties,' so

> [I]n the classical Islamic theory of the state, law and government were kept largely separate from one another . . . By remaining resolutely focused on the individual the legal establishment forsook the politicization of the law; by avoiding inclusion of the law as an instrument of state policy, the political authorities passed up the opportunity to use law as a vehicle of political centralization.[12]

As with primitive people, Muslims traditionally refused state power over their lives. The kind of distinctions we find between 'then' and 'now', between the largely hidden and suppressed alternative political configurations and our contemporary situations, suggest a fundamental dichotomy. This can be variously characterized as the pre-Columbus era, the last five hundred years (for those concentrating on the civilizations of native peoples) and tradition and modernity (for those emphasizing the sacred, such as the perennialists and traditionalists).

But state power is almost invisible, as often is modernity, and so the fundamental dichotomy between anything today (government, media, religion) and then is not always perceived. One way to call attention to modern and state contexts is to draw on analyses which trace the radical changes influencing daily life. Writers like Mumford, Berman, Illich, Feyerabend, and Ellul show us a world where everything is called into question, where the questions of 'why do we do this' and 'why do we think this is normal' assume a particularly poignant note. The popular anti-hero Travis McGee meditates:

> I get this crazy feeling. Every once in a while I get it. I get the feeling that this is the last time in history when the offbeats like me will have a chance to live free in the nooks and crannies of the huge and rigid structure of an increasingly codified society. Fifty years from now I would be hunted down in the street. They would drill little holes in my skull and make me sensible and reliable and adjusted.[13]

In Foucault's lecture 'The Political Technology of Individuals',[14] a fundamental change in politics is seen with the process of defining the 'police' in the seventeenth and eighteenth centuries. He locates a book written in 1779 which is the 'first great systematic program of public health for the modern state'.[15] At the same moment, 'the French Revolution gives the signal for the great national wars of our days . . . meeting their conclusion or their climax in huge mass slaughters'.

While for Saint Thomas, the king should imitate God to lead men to the good life, and for Machiavelli, the art of politics is to increase the power of the prince, the aim of the modern state is to 'reinforce the state itself'.[16] This gives rise to a political arithmetic, a statistics which creates a calculus of power, where 'the individual exists insofar as what he does is able to introduce even a minimal change in the strength of the state, either in a positive or in a negative direction . . . And sometimes what he has to do for the state is to live, to work, to produce, to consume; and sometimes what he has to do is to die.'[17]

Without a calculus of demography, a statistics of population, what we now call politics—state, power, or government—had little to do with the daily life of traditional societies. With the calculus, the individual becomes the business of the state. From before his birth to after his death, the state is concerned with any increase or decrease the individual might confer on its aggregate power. The state has an interest in monitoring and deciding the fate of infants, educating children, intervening to protect them from parental abuse, immunizing them, and so on. What rational opposition can there be, where one must argue today for 'freedom from state interrogation' over 'health' and 'saving lives'?

The desire of the modern state, which is to endlessly interrogate and govern the subject interminably, with forms that need to be filled out, credit card records, and social security numbers, is contrasted with the reticent 'primitive'. Resistance to development is a resistance to this interrogation.

The very idea of 'naked' truth, and truth 'laid bare' rests in a world-view quite opposite to that of the classical Muslim scholars. Now, the truth of someone is that person's failing, sins, and frailties. In the Islamic world, one did not broadcast shortcomings. In his discussion of the metaphor of rinsing the mouth and sniffing water in the process of *taharah* (ritual purity), Ibn al-Arabi reveals the typical emphasis given to this civilizational value. 'Even if his recompense (for speaking of evil),' Ibn al-Arabi comments, 'is in His statement, [*Allah loves not that evil should be noised abroad in public speech, except where injustice has been done*], [4:148], nevertheless silence about it is most excellent.'[18]

The resistance of the primitive is well-illustrated in a passage in Munif's novel about the advent of oil exploration in what is now Saudi Arabia, where the bureaucrats say, 'The information we need is simple and necessary, and it is confidential too.' To their long series of questions about his parents, Ibrahim blurts out 'What do you want with my mothers?' And then after even more questions, 'What's wrong with you—can't you talk about anything but my father and mother?' Finally, he cries out, 'God help me—leave me alone!'[19]

Communities who refuse statehood and states are found throughout the world, from the Penans in Malaysia to the Aborigines in Australia, from Indian nations throughout North, Central, and South America to Kurds and Pathans in South and Southwest Asia. *Cultural Survival Quarterly* reports that three-fourths of the 120 military conflicts in the world in 1987 were native nations defending themselves against nation-states.[20] The ultimate supremacy of the nation-state is not yet established and many communities throughout the world are struggling against it till death. In a world dominated by state powers, and at least—if not more—as influentially by corporations, it is no wonder that the voice of the ulema is seldom heard.

II. Caliphal Politics

What I am suggesting is that we should bypass the typical analysis of caliphate and sultanate as proto-states or as the central political arena in Islam; instead, the domain of the *fiqh* is much better suited for political analysis.

The classical discussions of caliphate are sparse, overly abstract, and full of hidden agendas. They are not very helpful while questioning how authority is configured in Islamic societies.[21] The voluminous discussions of who is best suited for leadership (*imamah*) during the prayer (*salah*), in contrast, is very helpful.[22]

Should it not then be possible to extrapolate from the discussion of the *salah*, ideas about a larger universe? Is not the ideal leader for the *salah*, the ideal leader for the larger society? Is not the discussion of the criteria for a good leader for the *salah* at the same time a discussion of the good leader of society? If indeed we can examine the *salah* as a microcosm of the Muslim universe, a number of propitious consequences ensue.

What I am proposing here is nothing short of an entire re-evaluation of politics in Islam. The entire fundamentalist discourse on the Islamic state in fact arises from the invisible concealment of a traditional world-view having its own kind of politics, by a modern world-view of the sovereign state. Let us therefore delve into this matter of politics, because one of the main reasons of examining the *fiqh* discussion of the *salah* as a microcosm for the larger discourse of Islamic communities, which is so propitious, stems from the reassessment of politics which it occasions.

Historically, there is a noticeable absence of sustained and direct discussion on Islamic leadership. The subject matter of kingship or caliphate tended to create treatises at once highly abstract and overly specific. The works of Mawardi, Nizam al-Mulk, al-Ghazali, and Ibn Khaldun, for example, when addressing kingship or caliphate, have quite definite agendas to pursue; attacking amid abstract and idealistic verbiage, a powerful woman behind a would-be leader, or simultaneous caliphates, or justifying pinning one's hopes on converting a ravaging Hun. Arkoun lists what Mawardi overlooks:

> Al-Mawardi talks neither of the Shi'ite theory of the designation of the caliph based on a text, nor of the great conflict (*al-fitna*) between Ali and Muawiya, nor of Yazid who, according to the Shi'ite version, had Hussein assassinated at Karbala, nor of the conditions of civil war which initiated the fall of the Umayyeds and the ascendance of the Abbasides, nor of the politics of Mamun toward the Mutazilites and to Shi'ism, nor that of Mutawakkil for installing Sunnism, nor of the conquest of power by the Buyides.[23]

The actual caliphate was formally abolished by Ataturk in 1925, and even though it was obvious that the caliphate had been an extremely ineffective system for decades, even centuries, the loss of the caliphate had a tremendous impact on Muslims throughout the world. Muslims in India, for example, spontaneously arose and began walking to Turkey to recover their world. Ali Abd al-Raziq's short treatise, published in Egypt in 1933 on government in Islam, arguing that the caliphate is not essential to the Islamic community, quickly brought him major troubles and seemed to many to be salt thrown on their wounds. To this day, many Muslims have put their hopes in a revived caliphate. We have a situation here where there is a dearth of material on Islamic government, together with an inchoate understanding that, against Abd al-Raziq, politics is essential to Islam.

The problem, as I see it, is that there is no state in Islam—state being understood in the Western sense of a sovereign, corporate institution with a reality across time and space, independent of its human constituents or components.[24] When people talk of the 'Islamic theory of state', Ayubi notes,

> [T]hey are addressing themselves specifically to the problem of government and especially to the conduct of the ruler, and not to the state as a generic category or to the body-politic as a social reality and a legal abstraction . . . Even when the Islamic bureaucracy developed and became quite complex, officials and other 'public' personnel appointed to certain jobs or dismissed from them, never signed a contract with the 'State' or any other 'moral personality', but simply with a certain individual employer (*al-muwalli*).[25]

The issue is not one merely of definition. The concept of a sovereign, corporate nation-state entails absolutism and totalitarianism—no matter how much people in liberal democracies want to believe that their freedom and rights are protected. Traditional scholars spoke of this kind of politics as Thoreau did, where the best government is the least government, or none at all. Ayubi writes that neo-fundamentalists 'invoke the text and quote the source, but in doing so they are highly selective and remarkably innovative. Political precedence is of practically no interest to them; neither is the main body of official jurisprudence, apart from a few exceptions such as Ibn Taimiya.'[26]

We tend to equate politics with state and government, and thus when we ask about politics in Islam, we are actually asking about states and governments.[27] At that point, we gather the fairly small series of works, like al-Mawardi's, discussing the caliphate and the sultanate, which digress into discussions about intact testicles and other criteria for leadership, and end up with Abd al-Raziq's ultimate destruction of the whole thing, with his persuasive argument that the Prophet left no system of government and Muslim scholarship never actually addressed the entire issue of how a people should be governed.

The moment we disengage 'politics' from 'state', an entirely new situation arises. The many Muslims who were appalled at Abd al-Raziq's position, and at all subsequent liberal positions on government, were right but they were inarticulate (the actual official rebuttal to his work seems to have zeroed in on his use of 'Bolshevik' in a long list of possible governmental systems which could be seen as Islamic). If we ask, 'What governmental system did the prophet leave his community?' the answer is 'the *fiqh* of the shariah'. If the shariah is the politics of the Islamic community, then its entire legal discussion—the *fiqh*—is the expression of politics in Islam. And whereas we have a few hundred pages on the subject matter of caliphate and sultanate, we have perhaps a million pages on the subject matter of *fiqh*.[28]

So if we want to examine Muslim views on leadership, power, relations with the other, differences in communities, structures, and institutions, we would do well to pass over the official statements on caliphates and sultanates and turn instead to the actual arena of political contention and discussion—the *fiqh*. Taking the selection of a leader for the *salah* to be a microcosm of political leadership in Islam unleashes a torrent of positions, arguments, ideas, and terminologies which begin to reflect the historical realities of politics in Islam. At the same time, it offers Muslims an authentic discursive format which allows for an Islamic assessment of politics today. The basic need, then, is to re-evaluate this *fiqh*, both for historical understandings as well as for contemporary problems.

III. The *Fiqh*

So what exactly is the *fiqh*? It is perhaps the most concrete and voluminous monument of Islamic civilization, one format of Muslim understanding (*tafaqquh*, f.q.h.)[29] of the shariah, the rules and regulations of Islam. Although the *fiqh* can become atrophied and reified, static and full of the weight of authority, it is traditionally the living expression of the Muslim community's commitment to realize the guidance of the shariah. For the Muslim, 'right life' is a consequence of right action, and the criterion for right belief is right conduct. Hence the importance of *fiqh*.

The *fiqh* combines concern with both the spiritual and the quotidian, and serves as the arena for political-economic life, regulating activity in the markets, mediating disputes, and determining David Easton's 'authoritative allocation of value', as well as administering rites of passage (birth, puberty, marriage, death). Its tendency for accumulation means that it preserves centuries of deliberations, discussions, decisions, and debates.

Therefore, the extension of the *fiqh*, and specifically the *fiqh* of *salah*, to the macrocosm allows us to reconstruct a political discourse. The *fiqh* surrounding the issue of privacy and windows, for example, tells us something about the priorities of Muslim scholars. We can reconstruct that when someone created a window, the neighbour's right of privacy prevailed: the existence of filled-in windows in traditional Muslim cities is the physical sign of the following event. Someone opens up a window to improve his house, and a neighbour begins to worry that the window looks into his house, disturbing his privacy; they take their case to the *qadi* (from the Arabic root q.d.y. as we saw, meaning to settle or resolve). The *qadi* seeks *sulh*, harmony among disputants, and so he brings along a builder to the site. If indeed the window 'harms'—from the axiomatic *hadith* 'There shall be no harming, nor being harmed', *la darar wa la dirar*—the window is boarded up.[30] I suggest that in this process, the traditional politics for Muslim societies is seen.

In this process, obedience to the revelation is manifested within community relationships. This is why a break between spirituality, as expressed in obedience to the revelation, and politics, as depicted in interactions in communities, is inconceivable in traditional Islam. Let us look now explicitly at spirituality and politics.

Notes

1. 'May Allah bless him and give him peace.' The blessing has spiritual value as fulfilling a command of Allah to those who believe: transliterated, it may allow the reader to 'glide' over without being distracted, as indeed it is generally not distracting in Islamic texts.
2. Many scholars decry the ulema and then praise some of them, such as Abu Hanifah or Malik or Shafii. Those who flocked to the state throughout history are not included here as ulema. Ibn al-Arabi tells this story: 'When the winds of caprice dominate over souls and the learned seek high degrees with kings, they leave the clear path and incline toward far-fetched interpretations. Thus they are able to walk with the personal desires of the kings in that within which their souls have a caprice, and the kings can support themselves by a shariah command . . . Al-Malik reported to me, after we had discussed such things, as follows . . . not a single ugly thing happens without the legal pronouncement of a jurist . . . "A jurist named so and so," and he specified for me the most excellent jurist of his country in religion and mortification, "gave me a pronouncement that it is not necessary to fast during the month of Ramadan itself." On the contrary, what is obligatory for me is fasting during one month of the year, and I can choose it myself. "So," said the Sultan, "I cursed him inwardly and did not show that to him. He is so and so," and he named him for me. God have mercy on all of them!' Translated by William C. Chittick (1989). *Ibn al-Arabi's Metaphysics of Imagination: The Sufi Path of Knowledge* (Albany: SUNY) 202. We might note the fact that the king did not rebuke the jurist, but let him persist, which gives an additional suggestion of the anger of the king, because without rebuke, the jurist is less likely to seek forgiveness (that is, *istighfar*) and more likely to meet harsh punishment in the next world.

3. Norbert Wiener (1954). *The Human Use of Human Beings: Cybernetics and Society* (New York: Avon Books).
4. I was impressed by his book *Four Arguments for the Elimination of Television* (Morrow/Quill, 1977) and wrote an article reflecting on its ideas: 'Is This (Fire) a Fake?' Mediated Experience, TV, and the Perception of Reality. In *Islamic Quarterly*, 35.3, (1991).
5. Oren Lyons, in Jerry Mander (1991). *In the Absence of the Sacred* (Sierra Club Books).
6. Lawrence Rosen (1989). *The Anthropology of Justice: Law as Culture in Islamic Society* (Cambridge: Press Syndicate).
7. Lawrence Rosen (1989).
8. William A. Graham's definition of Islamic traditionalism is, 'the widespread Muslim emphasis upon the primary, dual authority of the revelations of the Quran and the tradition or practice (Sunna) ascribed to the Prophet and the first few generations of Muslims (the pious forebears, *as-salaf*)' in Graham (1993). Traditionalism in Islam: An Essay in Interpretation. *Journal of Interdisciplinary History* 23,3:500.
9. The word Arab will refer to that language which was used before and during the descent of the Quran. The later generations used a language I will call Arabic. The former language is fixed and transcendentalized by the revelation, whereas the latter is a growing, living language which incorporates concepts and world-views which are not necessarily Islamic.
10. Quotations from Ibn Manzur are from his great dictionary, *Lisan al-Arab*, the 'Language of the Arab'.
11. See S. Parvez Manzoor (1991). The Future of Muslim Politics: Critique of the 'fundamentalist' theory of the Islamic State, *Futures* (April), where he notes that, 'Ironically, thus, though modern Sunni fundamentalism regards itself as an inheritor of the Ibn Taymiyan legacy, it capitally misses the focal point of his revivalist message. Reversing the position held by him with regard to the nature of statehood in Islam, modern fundamentalism proclaims the primacy of the state in Islam and accords it a status higher than that of the community.' Ayubi confirms Ibn Taymiyyah's position, commenting that 'Ibn Taimiya was among the exceptional ones: by ranking the integrity of the shariah higher that the unity of the umma, he was prepared to condemn the ruler if he did not live up to the ideological ideal. It is little wonder that he spent most of his life (and died) in prison.' Ayubi (1991). *Political Islam: Religion and Politics in the Arab World* (New York: Routledge).

12. Rosen (1989).
13. John D. MacDonald (1964). *The Quick Red Fox* (New York: Ballantine Books).
14. Michel Foucault (1988). *Technologies of the Self* (Massachusetts: The University Press).
15. Ibid.
16. Ibid.
17. Ibid.
18. *Futuhat al-Makkiyyah*, critical edition of Uthman Yahya.
19. Abdelrahman Munif (1989). *Cities of Salt* (New York: Vintage).
20. See Mander (1991).
21. One description of the criteria of caliphate is as follows: 'the leader is required to possess certain physical, psychological/moral and social/philosophical qualities. Sunni scholars have generally agreed that the caliph should be of sound mind and body; he should also demonstrate justice, dedication, courage, knowledge and competence in his role as the administrator of communal affairs. The doctrine is explicitly exclusive in the sense that it disqualifies females and non-Qurayshites from performing leadership roles.' Mehran Tamadonfar (1989). *The Islamic Polity and Political Leadership* (Boulder: Westview). The difficulties of trying to extract meaningful political truths from the classical discussions of *khalifah* and *imamah*, and fundamentalist preferences from leaders, is clear in both Tamadonfar's work and my dissertation, *The Ontological Status of Politics in Islam* (University of South Carolina, 1988). An examination of Muhammad Abduh, Mawdudi, Sayyid Qutb, and their like, tells us a lot about Muslim feelings of weakness before an ascendant, imperial West, but little about the actual workings of Muslim communities. Similarly abstract descriptions of the ideal President of the USA—perhaps brave, courageous, kind, knowledgeable, popular, handsome—would tell us little about politics on the ground.
22. Muhammad Arkoun focuses on Quranic axioms as the basis for an understanding of Islamic politics, a focus which he trains on the category of literature called 'ethics' (e.g., *Uyun al-akhlaq* and *Makarim al-akhlaq*), as well as 'the corpus of Sunni and Shi'ite, the treatises on *usul al-din* and *usul al-fiqh*, the rich literature of juristic discussions like the *Fatawa* of Ibn Taymiyyah, the *Miyar* of al-Wansharisi. All of the technological and juridical literature rests, as we have seen, on the Quranic axiology.' Arkoun (1986). *L'Islam, morale et politique* (Paris: United Nations).

23. Arkoun (1989).
24. Parvez Manzoor observes that for al-Ghazali, and this 'is representative of the entire body of juristic thought,' 'his commitment is to the civil society of Islam, the social order of the Muslim community, rather than to any polity that may be called the Islamic state.' Manzoor (1991).
25. Ayubi (1991).
26. Ibid.
27. Ayubi falls into the same trap as Abd al-Raziq, confirming that the Quran and *hadith* 'have very little to say on matters of government and the State.' Ayubi (1991). He goes on to talk of the problem of succession after the Prophet's death, so one assumes that the above statement restricts 'matters of government and the State' to succession. But what a restriction! And when one opens up, even slightly, the realm of 'the political', we find the Quran and *hadith* loquacious indeed. Ayubi says that what we have is that Islam is premised on 'the *collective* enforcement of *public* morals' (emphasis added), something he seems to think is not 'political'.
28. At least with the qualification 'if translated into English', because a single manuscript page of Arabic may require five to ten or even fifteen pages of printed translation. Adding up the printed works, and then including manuscripts in Cairo, Istanbul, Delhi, Hyderabad, and so on would certainly reach an awesome number of pages written about *fiqh* or the politics of Islam.
29. Arabic words have roots which are generally three letters, and by giving the root in the form 'f.q.h.' one knows that *fiqh* comes from the root 'f.q.h.' For example, *kitab* (book), *kataba* (he wrote), and *katib* (writer) are all classified as k.t.b.
30. The way a living *fiqh* was used to create harmonious, beautiful, and comfortable cities is illustrated in the book by Besim Selim Hakim's (1986). *Arabic-Islamic Cities* (New York: Routledge and Kegan Paul).

Chapter 2

Spirituality and the *Fiqh*

The attack on the *fiqh* by modern movements, such as fundamentalism, includes an attack on spiritual things as well. Western scholarship on Islam is beginning to recognize that traditionally the majority of the ulema participated in one or more Sufi paths.[1] For them, the concept of *ilm*, of sapiential knowledge, meant an integration between virtue, praxis, knowledge, and sanctity, just as it meant the integration of law and spirituality. One problem which particularly disturbs me in contemporary Muslim life, is that of the separation of law from spirituality and vice versa. There are Muslims who elevate their spiritual life beyond the concerns of their daily lives and discard law as an essentially mundane, rigid, and trivializing discipline. Then there are Muslims who have reified the law, taking a static and arid lump of rulings as the last word on a dead revelation. I would like to explore here the world-view which maintained an integration of law and spirituality and offer encouragement to those who work for a reintegration of shariah, *fiqh*, and spirituality.

The world-view which sustained the traditional Sufi scholars posited the following scenario. The essence of Islam is the shariah. The messenger of Allah, Muhammad, was sent as a mercy to the worlds and a demonstrator of the shariah. The *fiqh* is the application of the shariah to different times and places based on deeply and vigorously debated rules and methodologies (e.g., the *usul al-fiqh*). Spirituality is sought and expressed within the confines of the shariah boundaries. This world-view maintained Islamic communities through hundreds of years. It is my hope that by engaging the areas of law and spirituality, once again, in an integrated discursive system like the *fiqh* we may achieve some degree of integration, where our physical and worldly lives are perfected through our imaginal and spiritual lives; or to say it another way, our spiritual lives are perfected through our physical lives.

The classical ulema have a very clear idea of how divine guidance is to be applied and realized in communities. The importance of knowledge of language is seen in such works as the fourteenth century Ibn Manzur's *Lisan al-Arab*, where he creates, Noah-like, an ark to contain the words in circulation during the time of the Prophet and massive works identifying his Companions. In it, as many details of their lives as possible are assembled to enable the *hadith* scholar to evaluate chains of transmission which testify to a very particular structure of knowing—developed and maintained by an amorphous knowledge elite, the ulema. Their vision is by no means the only possible vision—its formal structure did not appear until three or more generations after the death of the Prophet. So while that vision is often either assumed as obvious, or rejected equally out of hand, I prefer to identify its implicit values and its normative force. Once we recognize its normative position, we immediately begin to identify its challengers. Three groups especially have been seen by the ulema as threatening and illegitimate.

I. The Khawarij, Batiniyyah, and Ibahiyyah Types

These three groups are present today, so one may speak of types. First is the Khawarij challenge. Historically, this is the group which sought a radical Islam, shorn of its cultural, linguistic, and human accoutrements. It is this group which could contemplate the murder of Uthman, draw a definition of 'Muslim' so tight as to wage war on slackers or Muslims not up to their standards. This group in its later incarnations could destroy the tombs of the Prophet and companions, as the Wahhabis did. Their orientation towards the future and their vision of movement and progress make this type peculiarly modern. Their ideology makes it desirable to erase centuries of learning and tradition (going directly to Quran and Sunna, they ignore and denigrate centuries of Muslim scholarship). This type, as it manifests itself in modern fundamentalism, creates clear lines of battle, quickly and surely defining its enemies (Jews, tradition-bound Muslims, Americans), seeks rapid development and success (throwing derision at the traditional responses of *sabr* [patience], and the other-worldliness of Sufis), and mocks the sacred, whether in art, attire, housing, or occupation.

Ibn Manzur emphasizes their tendency to restrict and make the religion hard and harsh. Among the Khawarij, there is another group called Haruriyyah—a name based on their locale. Ibn Manzur says, 'al-

Harura is a place outside of Kufah to which is related the Haruriyyah, belonging to the Khawarij, because al-Harura was the first place they founded their community, and the place where they declared their authority after they opposed Ali.' He then goes on to describe how the word is adjectivally used: 'The linguistic extension is, "Someone is Harurawi." ' He then quotes al-Jawhari, who said, 'al-Harura is a name of a village.' The word also appears in a *hadith* from Aishah when she was questioned about the menstruant making up the *salah.* Ibn Manzur says, 'She replied, "Are you a Haruriyyah?" They are the Haruriyyah belonging to the Khawarij who fought against Ali. On their part they used to make harsh that which in the religion was an easing, so when Aishah saw this woman making the affairs of menstruation harsher, she compared her to the Haruriyyah. They make their affairs harsher in many of their issues, and they torment themselves with them. It is said they want to oppose the Sunna and leave the [local] community just as they left the [larger] community of the believers.'

Groups which make their religion more difficult and demanding in order to distinguish themselves from the larger body of Muslims fit this type.

A second group are the Batiniyyah, a word based on *batin*, the inward, who denigrate the body and the material. Ibn al-Arabi describes their error in this passage:

> Know that Allah addressed humankind in his totality and did not honour his outwardness over his inwardness, nor his inwardness over his outwardness. They are dedicated, the ones who invite people [to the religion], most of them, to knowledge of the *ahkam* [legal properties] of the *shar* (cf. shariah) in their outwardness, but are heedless of the *ahkam* set down by revelation in their inwardness, except for the few, and they are folk on Allah's path. They investigate that, outwardly and inwardly. There is no *hukm* [legal property] which they determine according to the revelation, for their outwardnesses, except they see that that *hukm* has a relationship to their inwardnesses. They take, in that way, the entirety of the *ahkam* of the revealed religions. They worship Allah with that which He made *shar* for them, outwardly and inwardly, and they succeed where the majority fail.

Continuing, Ibn al-Arabi says,

> Three groups arose, one misled and another making others misled. One takes the *ahkam* of the shariah and discharges them for their inwardnesses, and they leave nothing of the *ahkam* of the shariah for their outwardnesses. They are called Batiniyyah, and they are, in that, in different schools. Imam

> Abu Hamid [al-Ghazali] indicated, in his book *Kitab al-Mustazhiri*[2] refuting them, something of their schools and explained their errors therein.

Summing up, Ibn al-Arabi says,

> Felicity is with outward folk. They are diametrically opposite inward folk. But felicity, all felicity, is with the group who combine the outward and inward; they are ulema (knowers) of Allah and His *ahkam*.[3]

Although there is a historical identification by Sunnis of the Ismailis as the Batiniyyahs, this tendency is found among many scholarly and progressive Muslims, who have intellectualized, abstracted, and made philosophical and symbolic, their approach to the sacred text.

A third group may be called the Ibahiyyah, the ones who make everything permissible, denying divine punishment, and relativizing all actions.

The Khawarij voice is the fundamentalist voice which commands a great audience, and not just because of the Western media. The secularist or liberal voice, which has elements of Batiniyyah and Ibahiyyah, gets its amplification from a cosy relationship with liberalist yearnings in the West and political power in the East.[4]

Since one could hardly imagine a Muslim who claimed not to believe in the fundamentals of Islam, fundamentalist is not a very apt description. Let me introduce the term 'technist' for the Khawarij tendency as it appears today.

A technist is a Muslim who believes fervently that the historical decline of Muslims is due to a problem of technique: if only Muslims had correctly applied such and such a technique, they would not be suffering today in Bosnia, Somalia, Palestine, and elsewhere. And if only Muslims would apply another technique (e.g., 'be as brothers unto one another', or apply the *hijab*, or the *hudud* as in the Hudood Ordinances in Pakistan), we would be as successful as the Israelis or Americans or Japanese. The ultimate in technist thinking is the notion that the Quran is a constitution, reducing, as only technists can do, a sacred text into a tremendously uni-dimensional and flat document.

One consequence of the text produced by the technists is that they have in effect co-opted the revelation and the *fiqh*. Well-meaning Muslims, Sufis and spiritualists, lay and non-academically trained Muslims alike, tend to accept the technist arrogation of the texts without challenge. Believing themselves bereft of *hadith* and the Quran, they forsake the text and search elsewhere for solutions to the problems facing their communities.

The contemporary Batiniyyah and Ibahiyyah viewpoints have accepted the primacy of the modern world-view. Now, in order to live in this world, they must derive a means of handling the Islamic text. The means derived often revolve around a rejection of literal and narrow-minded interpretations and an emphasis on a moral and ethical Islam distanced from its historical roots.

I went through a period, as one of those well-meaning Muslims, where I too believed that the technists had dominion over the texts, and that our only hope was in recapturing an ethical Islam beyond the texts. But I first sought to challenge the technists on their own turf. I found that the technists had in effect, created an understanding of Islam which is fundamentally divergent from that of a dozen centuries of scholarship, that understanding of Islam manifested in traditional architectures, languages, and poetry. The kings of innovation, I soon found, were the self-styled heirs of Ibn Taymiyyah and Ibn Hanbal, whereas my study of these thinkers leads me to believe that they completely rejected all manifestations of this Khawarij tendency.

The most literal reading of the Quran I have ever come across is that of Ibn al-Arabi, a figure condemned by many groups, and who was until recently read by Western scholarship precisely because of his unorthodox opinions.

Let me, as an aside, point to a wonderful discussion of Ibn al-Arabi found in Michel Chodkiewicz's recent book.[5] In this book, Chodkiewicz reminds us that Ibn Hajar al-Asqalani remarked perplexedly that at first Ibn al-Arabi was received quite enthusiastically among the folk of the Sunna. Vilification of Ibn al-Arabi was a later phenomenon, and one which repeated itself recently in the Egyptian parliament where the vilifiers, without reading him themselves, attacked concepts like *wahdat al-wujud* which are not found in Ibn Arabi's own writings. They were, and are, in effect, attacking the eastern Ibn al-Arabi. But although Chodkiewicz demonstrates that Ibn al-Arabi is possibly the most literal interpreter of the text of Quran and Sunna, and that Ibn al-Arabi's *fiqh* is integral to his entire vision, he does not suggest that conventional ulema will love him for this. One well might ask, where is this Ibn al-Arabi?

Chodkiewicz's answer is that Ibn al-Arabi's ideas are very much alive and well in Sunni circles. Instead of looking for the great literature left by the eminent Shi'ite scholars, one must look for the diffusion of basic concepts of Ibn al-Arabi's works. Employing their own *taqiyyah* (dissimulation), the Sunni ulema tended to revile or ignore Ibn al-Arabi in broad public spheres while teaching him in private circles. Founders of the Sufi paths were able to pass on complete systems of spiritual journeying by relying on the articulate foundation laid by Ibn al-Arabi. Local shaikhs and Sufis gained access to Ibn al-Arabi's works through his popularizers, like Sharani. Chodkiewicz's description of this diffusion is fascinating, as he takes the reader through this *zawiyah*, Sufi centre's library, to the stories of that local saint, finding resonances of Ibn al-Arabi's thought throughout.

Another great contribution is Chodkiewicz's characterization of the importance of the shariah in Ibn al-Arabi's vision. He writes, 'Charisma, sciences, epiphanies, all the signs and all the accomplishments are attached to the *faraid*, and thus to the law.'[6] And he quotes Ibn al-Arabi, 'If that (that God becomes the hearing, the sight of the servant [in the *hadith qudsi*]) is the fruit of supererogatory acts, just think about the fruit of obligatory acts!' Instead of dichotomy, 'Thus appears another case of the coincidence of *zahir* and *batin*. The spiritual quest is completed through that by which it was started: observance of the shariah.'

This coincidence of outward and inward paths, this 'completion' of the spiritual quest through the shariah is entirely missed by the technists, even though we conventionally accept their claim that they are interpreting the Quran and Sunna literally. But in fact, technists are purely modern, incorporating unawares, notions and world-views fundamentally at odds with traditional Islamic world-views.

The views of technists concerning man and caliphate, for example, are utterly modern. For centuries the Quranic commentaries restricted the entire caliphate complex, described in the Quran, to Adam and the other prophets. Suddenly, due to the attractiveness of an all-powerful modern Western man, technists were saying that we are all supposed to assume caliphate. This ultra-modern sleight of hand allows technical Islamicists to paint an Islamic facade over newly industrializing countries' efforts to gain power and prestige, to treat nuclear weapons as a simple Islamic progression from swords and arrows, and to explain why modern Muslims are wielding such power over environments and peoples whereas traditional Muslims were wallowing in passive and unaggressive relationships with others and with nature.

If their nation-states are caught in neo-colonial nets, then it must be because the leaders are not ideal. Logically, if you could install ideal leaders, you would avoid all problems. So the search for a caliph who will forcefully implement the shariah—whose politics must be absolute because they are linked to absolute religion—preoccupies the technists.

Ironically, the traditional view is that caliphate is preceded by absolute servanthood to the divine, such that the only person qualified to lead is the one who is so effaced that the divine rules through him as a marionette is led by the puppeteer. One recalls the admonishment to His messenger in the Quran, *It is not you who killed them: it was Allah who killed them; and you did not throw when you threw, but Allah threw* (8:17). Ibn al-Arabi's metaphor for this is the *hadith qudsi*, that is, a *hadith* of Allah's words, '. . . I am his ear with which he hears . . .'

For centuries the scholars of commentary have interpreted (13:11) *Verily Allah does not change what is with a people until they change themselves* as meaning, 'Verily Allah does not change what is with a people [by way of good] [to bad] until they change themselves [by doing bad, and so become deserving of punishment]'. For example, al-Razi's commentary on this part of the verse is as follows.

> As for His statement, may He be exalted, *Verily Allah does not change what is with a people until they change what is with themselves*, the word of all the commentators indicates that the meaning of *will not change* is what is with them by way of good fortune to the descent of vengenance, unless there are among them people of disobedience and wickedness. Al-Qadi said, there is no other possible meaning except this one . . . since He, may He be exalted, begins with good fortune in *din* [religious matters] and *dunya* [worldly matters], and then blesses in that whom He will . . . Al-Qadi [also] raises the issue that He does not visit punishment on the children of the polytheists due their fathers since they have yet not changed what is with themselves by way of good fortune.

Today, of course, the interpretation is quite the opposite, implying that if only we will change ourselves—become punctual, brotherly, and technically correct—God will make us successful, like the Americans or the Japanese.

These modern technical interpreters are not literal, nor do they have any special claims to authencity.[7] They entirely dispense with the connecting chain (*silsilah*) which links ourselves to the prophetic period, seeking to tear out the revealed data onto their supposed *tabula rasa*. In fact, by claiming to consider only the Quran and Sunna—which they do not do literally nor very well—they ignore the inevitable cultural baggage they bring. And this baggage, quite clearly, was packed in the West. By sweeping away centuries of Islamic civilization, they claim to approach the texts literally. They reject previous scholarships, legal schools, and spiritual paths.

They claim to take just from the Quran and Sunna, effectively denying the interpretive process and so erect for themselves an unassailable stance. The way to challenge this stance is to demonstrate that they do indeed, bring with them their modern baggage, their televisions and computers, their ache for industrial power and prestige, and their frustration with female suffrage and universal education, thereby coming to conclusions utterly at odds with a thousand years and more of commentary on the Quran.

It is impossible to give credence to someone who takes a Quranic verse, especially in translation, and says 'so and so' is what it means. To be authentic, a discussion of a verse or a *hadith* must be prefaced by references to classical commentaries. This does not necessarily preclude novel interpretations, but it discourages the arrogance of believing that fourteen centuries of devoted Muslim scholarship missed something we only now see.

I started applying this process after talking with a traditionally educated, Ph.D. scholar of Islamic history. He was teaching commentary and some of his students were talking to me about a verse with political implications, the command to fight non-Muslims. Intrigued, I talked with their teacher. I asked him what the answer was, what the correct interpretation was. He said he had found dozens of different opinions, all of them firmly within the bounds of Islamicity, all of them authentic. He went on to offer a picture of 'abrogated-abrogating' verses that turned me decisively away from a technical understanding of Islam.

The answer of course, is that it is all contextual and interpretive. It is the Muslims who are striving to respond to the divine commands, to live a life of sacred obedience, to produce on earth—as much as He wills—a just society. The way we accomplish what is good, is by engaging at every step our understanding of the divine revelation. *Fiqh*, then, is one of the means we have of following, of engaging, the guidance of the Quran and Sunna. The *fiqh* has its rules of engagement, its courtesies, and protocols for disagreement, its systems of logic and demonstration; it has its rules of citation and chains of authority which are evaluated intellectually, not charismatically.

The Islamic life is not a technique. Nor is it an abstract ethics, a vague desire to 'do good'. It is rather the manifestation of guidance, the strides we take for ourselves and in society to follow the straight path. One beauty of Islamic civilization is that so many scholars have expressed a number of positions and interpretations. While this dismays the technist, it emboldens those who wish to realize the general divine command for their particular situation.

One example of a *fiqh* discussion which rejects the reifying and reductionist machinations of technists can be found in the following case. For this issue, the *imamah* (prayer leadership) of a child, Ibn al-Arabi examines three different positions and gives a metaphor for each position.[8] There is quite clearly no one position which is absolutely better than the others. The issue is not one of the right answer, but one of delving more deeply into the case in order to find appreciation at the higher levels, instead of moving down to a least common denominator. In fact, in order to quiet inevitable conflicts in Muslim communities, some suggest we ignore the details of Islam and hold firmly to the bigger picture. Frithjof Schuon denounces this kind of exoteric ecumenism, writing that

> When a man seeks to escape from 'dogmatic narrowness' it is essential that it should be 'upwards' and not 'downwards': dogmatic form is transcended by fathoming its depths and contemplating its universal content, and not by denying it in the name of a pretentious and iconoclastic 'ideal' of 'pure truth'.

Or worse, as James Cutsinger adds, 'in the name of a tolerance whose chief objective is of a strictly social or political sort'. Schuon's metaphor is the false ecumenism where, 'to reconcile two adversaries, one strangles them both, which is certainly the best way to make peace.'[9]

Ibn al-Arabi's discussion follows.

> The [scholars of the *fiqh*] disagree about the leadership of the child, *sabiy* [s.b.y.] who is not mature, even though he is a reciter of the Quran. Some people permit that absolutely, and some people forbid that absolutely, and some people permit it for the supererogatory prayers, but not for the required *salah*.
>
> The crossover [from the outward ritual to the inward truth, but not vice versa] of the matter for that is, that one says, 'So and so childishly tends [s.b.y.] to something' when he inclines to it, and since the child inclines toward the property of Nature, and is swayed by his individual desires, he is called a child; meaning, he is inclined to his cravings. He is without maturity in respect to intellect, which is required for the prescription of the Law. Nature, in its standing, is without the intellect, so it is not correct for Nature to have priority, nor for the one who inclines to Nature to have priority, even if he is inclining to Nature by rights, so in fact Nature has the position of the one behind, and indeed [the one who inclines to Nature] is behind, and the one who is behind shall not be a leader standing in front: it is the opposite of what the property of leadership is about.
>
> So the one who considered *this* crossover did not permit the leadership of the child even if he is a reciter. And the one who considered the fact of his having memorized *hamil* [h.m.l.] the Quran, understood the leadership to be

> that of the Quran, not of the child-leadership to be subject to being followed on account of the Quran, so he permitted the leadership of the child. He said, 'We gave him[10] jurisdiction as a child' [19:12]—i.e., jurisdiction of leadership—and They said[11] 'How shall we talk to one who is in the cradle, as a child'? [The newborn infant Jesus] said, 'I am a slave of Allah; He gave me the Book and made me a prophet' [19:29-30]—and prophethood is the position of leadership, despite his being called a child.
>
> And the one who saw the worship of the child to be a free-will worship—in the absence of a prescription of the Law requiring him to do it—and who saw that the supererogatory prayers are a freely-willed act of worship, he permitted the *salah* of the child as the leader for the supererogatory prayers, but not the required prayer, due to the supererogatory prayers' relation to free-will.[12]

Thus, without seeking to create a new position, Ibn al-Arabi instead examines previous decisions and describes what Allah had disclosed for him about the truths behind the different positions. In fact, in the thousands of pages of text expounding Ibn al-Arabi's special understanding of the *fiqh* positions, he enumerates the various positions held historically by the ulema but usually indicates which of those positions he himself prefers and then illuminates the 'crossover' (from outward ritual to inward truth) involved in each case. As a result, one gains from this kind of study of the *fiqh* a deep understanding of the physical manifestation of following the commands, and at the same time bridges the inward and outward aspects of the revelation, affirming at once the necessity and value of strict obedience to the outward realm of ritual while grounding and authenticating the inward spirituality of the believer.

Notes

1. Graham notes that, 'for all of the varied forms that Sufi religiosity has taken and the often sharp critique Sufis have levelled against average piety and rote observance, major Sufi thinkers and leaders have seen themselves not so much as opponents of shariah-minded piety championed by the ulema, but more as proponents of an inner, esoteric, or simply more spiritual understanding and observance of the more 'external', exoteric, or orthoprax traditions of the shariah as codified and cultivated by the ulema. Similarly, many of the greatest legal and religious scholars within ulema scholarly traditions have been themselves also members of Sufi orders and written works important to both camps. Thus we must constantly guard against portraying the shari and Sufi traditions as mutually exclusive, closed communities, on the order of competing sects or "churches" ' Graham (1993).
2. Written for the Abbasid caliph al-Mustazhir (1094-1118), on the scandals of the Batiniyyah, *Kitab al-mustazhiri al-fadaih al-batiniyyah*. See Arthur Jeffrey (ed.) (1962). *A Reader on Islam*, for a translation of a part of this book, *On the Disgraceful Doctrines of the Esoteric Sects*.
3. *Futuhat*.
4. This relationship has its bizarre elements. In my review of a review of Hanafi's modernist Islam, I pointed out some of these elements. Kazuo Shimogaki, in *Between Modernity and Post-Modernity: The Islamic Left and Dr Hasan Hanafi's Thought: A Critical Reading* (1993, Japan: The Institute of Middle Eastern Studies, International University of Japan), argues that Hanafi's *The Islamic Left* is a form of resistance, however flawed, and proceeds to work from a quote from Foucault that, 'Where there is power, there is resistance, and yet, or rather consequently, this resistance is never in a position of

exteriority in relation to power.' But Shimogaki misreads this central tenet in Foucault's work. What Foucault is drawing attention to is the complicity of the victim and the oppressor, the intimate relationship of power that is created between the dominator and the dominated. There is the *ad hominem* argument that this insight of Foucault's is derived from his personal life. From what I understand, the victim who is tied up and abused is very much controlling his abuser, egging him on, revelling in forcing his torturer to beat harder. If this is so, one might speculate that there is a small but vocal portion of the Muslim world in some kind of twisted power play, at once affirming Muslim inferiority and Western superiority, saying we revel in the fact that you need us on the bottom so that you can be on the top. I applaud Shimogaki's use of postmodern thinkers, but these are strange companions indeed. And I realize once again that those vocal Muslims who are so enthralled at the military whip of the West, so impressed by the engorged size of its missiles, so shocked at its uncovered women, are intertwined with their enemy, locked in a strange and ugly embrace.

5. Michel Chodkiewicz (1993). *An Ocean Without Shore: Ibn Arabi, The Book, and the Law* (Albany: State University of New York).
6. This and the following quotes are from Chodkiewicz (1993).
7. Parvez Manzoor remarks that 'suffice to say at this juncture that like, "the Holy War", the notion of "the Islamic state" is not an authentic fact of Muslim cognition. It represents a remoulding of the Islamic metal in the alien consciousness of modernity.' Manzoor (1991).
8. The word here is *itibar* which is literally 'metaphor', but not necessarily as many now understand the word. 'To carry something beyond', is the literal meaning of the Greek *meta-phorein*, and for Ibn al-Arabi, the *itibar* or 'crossover' is the process of taking a truth in the outward realm and crossing it over into the inward realm. The act of crossing over does not denigrate either realm (nor does it destroy the bridge between them), but rather affirms and deepens the truth in both realms.
9. James S. Cutsinger (1992). 'A Knowledge That Wounds Our Nature: The Message of Frithjof Schuon' in *Journal of the American Academy of Religion* LX,3,1992:478.
10. That is, Jesus.
11. In the story related in 19:16-40, an angel is sent from God to Mary who announces the gift of a son; she has birth pains, but is given water to drink and dates to eat and is told not to talk to anyone, telling

any questioners that she has vowed not to speak to anyone on that day. To divert criticism of her for having born a child, she points to the infant Jesus.

12. *Futuhat*.

CHAPTER 3

Ibn al-Arabi and *Ijtihad*

Frank E. Vogel remarked that Western studies of Islamic law have 'often omitted, justifiably or not, any consideration of the law's application'.[1] This has led to confusion about concepts such as the 'closed gates of *ijtihad*', where, as Wael B. Hallaq noted, we get 'the oddity that scholars should declare *ijtihad* non-existent, while they at the very same time acclaim certain *fuqaha* of their own age as *mujtahids*, exercising *ijtihad*.'[2] Although Vogel gives an intriguing outline of an approach which should be used to address this and other issues, I believe there is much more than what meets the historical eye.

Discussions about *ijtihad* are in fact indications of deeply held political positions. Solving the question of *ijtihad* is therefore beyond the scope of a narrowly conceived historicity.

Vogel lists three 'peculiar tenets associated with the theory of *qada*',[3] which make the application of law problematic, but which also more deeply evince a radical and uncompromising world-view. First is the tenet that the *qadi* be a *mujtahid*, one able to do *ijtihad*. Second is that 'nothing but the revealed texts and the concrete facts of the case ought to constrain the *qadi's* conscience.'[4] And third that there can be no reversals or appeals of decisions based on *ijtihad* of the *qadi*. Vogel's notes that Ibn al-Muqaffa and others must have perceived that if 'this conception of *qada*—so idealistic, individualistic, multifarious, and unpredictable—were given full scope, Islamic legal systems would face great practical difficulty'.[5] Vogel, and a great number of legal scholars over the centuries, favour an 'Islamic legal system' over idealizing conceptions. There are thinkers, however, who do not do so, particularly Ibn al-Arabi, and it is their concept of *ijtihad* which we examine here.

Vogel correctly links this idealizing conception of *qada* to an endemic tension between the sultan and the state, which wants a standardized, centralized, and codified system of law that can be practiced universally with the power of the sultan/president. We can look at comments by al-Sharani in his *Mizan al-Kubra* which illustrates the inherent tension between the traditional, idealizing concept of *qada* and the desires of the sultan. He writes,

> Layth Ibn Sad, Allah be pleased with him, wrote to Imam Malik asking him about an issue, and Imam Malik wrote to him, 'O brother Imam, the *hukm* [determinative legal property] of Allah for this issue is what arose before you', and he said that only to show that each *mujtahid* [one who does *ijtihad*] is upon the source of the shariah which the *madhahib* [schools of jurisprudence] branch out from.[6]

He then relates paradigmatic stories surrounding state power confronting the legal discourse. The state is interested in codification, superficial unity, and arrogation of all coercive and punitive powers to itself. One of the stories begins with the perils of state *qadi*-ship as related, concerning Abd-Allah Ibn Wahhab, 'to whom the caliph wrote a letter to be a *qadi* in Egypt; he hid in his house, but some of them found him one day and said, O Ibn Wahhab, won't you come out and make the legal determination [*tahakkam*] between the people with the book of Allah and the Sunna of the messenger of Allah? He said, What! When I know that the ulema will gather with the prophets and the *qadis* with the sultans?'[7]

Imam Malik is thematically linked, by al-Sharani and others, to the anti-state world-view found periodically in the Muslim world. In a series of stories, that theme is developed.

> Harun al-Rashid came to Imam Malik (Allah be pleased with him), and said to him, 'Let me disseminate and publish this book which you attended to in the country of Islam, in order to bring the community together.' He said to him, 'O Amir of the believers, the disagreement of the ulema is a mercy from Allah on this community, so everyone is upon guidance and strives for Allah.'

In another story in the series, we read,

> And Harun al-Rashid wanted to put his book *al-Muwatta* on the Kabah and bring people to what was in it, and he said to him, 'Do not do so, because the companions of the messenger of Allah disagreed about the branches and dispersed to different countries, and each one is correct.'
>
> I heard our Shaykh al-Islam Zakariya, may Allah have mercy on him, saying that when Manzur did the *hajj*, he said to Imam Malik, 'I decided to command by your book which you produced, and it would be abrogating,

> and then I would propagate it to every city of the cities of the Muslims, and I would command them to practice it, and they would not refer to anything else.' Imam Malik said, 'Do not do so, O Amir of the believers, because the people have had handed over to them positions, and they heard *hadith* and they examined reports, and each peoples takes what was handed over to them, and they yield to Allah with it, so leave the people alone and what they choose for themselves in every country.'[8]

The desire of the ruler is to codify laws. The kind of application of shariah which Malik conceived is impossible for emerging states. The state is interested in one answer not multiplicity, in one mass not diversity, in efficiency and not variance. One tentative contact between those scholars who would aid the state in codification occurred within two centuries of the death of the Prophet. Vogel describes it as follows:

> [Ibn al-Muqaffa] recommended to the caliph that the latter examine all of the conflicting rulings on each issue, select among them, and then codify his choices into a written law. This proposal was defeated, and with it a bid that the ruler—wielding the authority of *siyasah* [political power] with its breadth, flexibility, responsiveness to utility, and, above all, powers of compulsion—should seize control of legislation and thereby replace the ulema and their rigorously individualistic and conscience-based *ijtihad*.[9]

However, other contacts succeeded a thousand years ago and the superstructure of *fiqh* became autonomous and fixed. The contact was genuine compromise. The sultans wanted a codified law which would place all the authority and legitimacy of Islam at their disposal, creating a system of law which would be efficient and centralized, maximizing of utility and concentrating all discipline and punishment under the sultan's or state's hand. The ulema wanted a *fiqh* which could be responsive to the highly diverse cultures and situations the Muslims found themselves in; a system which would maintain a hierarchy of knowledge, not a hierarchy of property or be subjugated to demands of efficiency over appropriateness; and a place in a community which sought their knowledge, tradition, and authority. The compromise reached was the 'closed door of *ijtihad*'.

The ulema severely constricted their massive *fiqh* superstructure until it was reduced to 589 issues.[10] They agreed that for these 589 issues they will proffer one position, which would be the representative position of their *madhhab*, school of jurisprudence. No one would be able to switch from one school to another and no one would be able to reopen the legal discourse first set by the founding Imams, even on evidence. They got the door shut on flagrant abuse of legal power by the sultan, while the latter got a codified law and a large degree of *siyasah*.

But it is my argument that many of the ulema, and especially the Sufi scholars,[11] were quite conscious of the sultan's and later the state's designs on Islamic law, and that they supported a conception of *qada* which, while causing great practical difficulty, was nevertheless essential to the meaningful life exhorted in Islam. They struggled explicitly to keep the authority of practising *ijtihad* located indigenously, and away from state power.

What is at stake in this debate? For Ibn al-Arabi, the denial of *ijtihad* amounts to nothing less than the denial of Allah's continuing, living solicitude and the mission of the Prophet as a mercy to the worlds. In one passage where Ibn al-Arabi talks about what we are calling the closed doors of *ijtihad*, he draws out in the starkest terms imaginable, the true location of *hukm*, which means property, ruling, and decision. The *hukm*, he says, belongs to Allah, not the intellect. When we do not know the property of a thing, we must rely on Allah. This act of relying on Allah is *ijtihad*, and entails becoming 'like the corpse in the hands of the washer', which is a definition of being an *abd* (a bondsman or slave) to Allah. When the *abd* achieves this radical passivity, it is as when Muhammad believed that he threw the sand, at the Battle of Badr, but it was Allah who throws—*You did not throw, when you threw, but Allah threw* (8:17), a verse which negates one thing, affirms one thing, and then affirms another thing.

Let us examine one of Ibn al-Arabi's discussions on this issue, found in his chapter on mysteries of *taharah* (purity), when he discusses wiping the shoes for *wudu*, when travelling, but with the added situation that there is a hole in the shoe. Ibn al-Arabi is going to use this particular *fiqh* issue (one of the 589) to demonstrate, again thematically, that it is Allah who Acts, something which orthodox and conventional ulema would entirely endorse, but in a way, which if they perceive, they would find highly dangerous. In particular, Allah Acts; the shariah has confirmed the *hukm* of the one who does *ijtihad*; so h/He a/Acts.[12]

As with all of Ibn al-Arabi's works, the original, fixed and transcendentalized Arab language is used; this is not the living language of Arabic. I use Ibn Manzur's (d. 711/1311) *Lisan al-Arab* to access this language. The first word we need is *khuff*. Ibn Manzur says, 'A person's *khuff* is what touches the ground from the *batin* [bottom] of one's *qadam*'.[13]

About *khafa* (kh.f.y.), a word that will be crucial for this passage, Ibn Manzur says, 'The *khafa* of the lightning is its sparks. And to kh.f.y.

something is to make it *zahir* [topside, outward, manifest], appear [z.h.r] and to bring it out. One says the downpour [kh.f.y.] the mice, when it brought them out from their burrows. Imru al-Qays said, describing horses [racing across the desert], *khafa-hunna [the horses] brought them out [the mice] from their burrows*).' And al-Lahyani said, 'If you keep the secret, we will not kh.f.y. it'. His word, *We will not kh.f.y. it* is, 'We will not make it *zahir*'. And the recitation of His word, '*Verily the Hour is coming, but I shall kh.f.y. it*' (20:15), means, 'I shall make it *zahir*', which al-Lahyani related from al-Kasai, Muhammad Ibn Sahl, and from Saiyd Ibn Jabir. And kh.f.y. something is to keep it concealed; kh.f.y. also means to make it *zahir*, and the two are opposites.. And *akhfaytu* (kh.f.y. 'I concealed') something means *satartu-hu* (s.t.r., 'I veiled it').

Ibn al-Arabi says,

> As for the *hukm* in the *batin* [inwardness], we call shoes *khuff* because of *khafa*, as the shoes completely veils [s.t.r.] the foot. So when the shoe is torn, and something of the foot becomes *zahir* [exposed], then wipe that part of the foot which is *zahir*, and wipe the shoe. And that only as long as it can be called a shoe—inevitably with this condition. Here is a strange mystery for the one with sharp understanding. The *khafa* is also the *zahir*! Imru al-Qays says, *khafa-hunna out of their tunnels,* that is, they brought them out and they made them *zahir*.

So in this passage we have the shoe connected to the word *khafa*, which includes the meaning of veiling something, with its act of veiling being the same definition used by al-Layth in Ibn Manzur's dictionary. We then have some part of the foot emerging, with the verb here being *zahara*, which is related linguistically to *zahir*, which is the antonym of *batin*, meaning contextually top and bottom or outward and inward. Ibn al-Arabi then noted the mysterious—but linguistically-based—connection of *khafy* and *zahir*.

Continuing, we find this:

> We argue for wiping what emerges, because we were commanded in the Book of Allah to wipe the feet,[14] so when something of the foot emerges, we wipe it.
>
> As for the inward realm, the outwardness of the shariah is a veil [*sitr*] over a reality of the *hukm* of unity [*tawhid*], in relating everything to Allah.

So, if everything is related to Allah, who is then left to be charged with performing the shariah? Ibn al-Arabi has a series of answers to this question which he explores throughout the *Futuhat*, but the fact is that certain kinds of descriptions of *tawhid* (oneness of God) are offensive, requiring an *adab* (courtesy) which attributes all good to Allah and all bad to oneself.[15]

Then, Ibn al-Arabi says:

> So the *taharah* concerning the shariah is connected and it is that you associate the *tawhid* of it with the fact, that you see it as a *hukm* of Allah in His creation, not a *hukm* of the things which belong to creation, like administrative wisdom.

We saw that the outwardness of the shariah veils the reality of *tawhid*. This reality of *tawhid* is related to the 'radical ambiguity of existence'. William Chittick writes that, 'the Quranic verse that Ibn al-Arabi cites more often than any other to show the radical ambiguity of existence was revealed after the battle of Badr, which turned in favour of the Muslims when the Prophet picked up a handful of sand and threw it in the direction of the enemy. Concerning the Prophet's throwing of this sand, the Quran says *You did not throw when you threw, but God threw* [8:17].' What this means in this passage is that the *taharah* of wiping of the shoe proceeds whether the veil is purified, the shoes or the foot recalling the authentic *hadith* of Allah that *Verily I become the foot of the abd* [*worshipper*] *with which he walks*.[16]

The word *abd* here is crucial, because it is the same station of *abd* which characterized Muhammad and which is recited in one version of the testimony: 'I testify that Muhammad is His *abd* and His messenger'. The station of this kind of *abd* is one which negates any semblance of independence and Lordship, and which consequently affirms that the speech (*kalam*) is Allah's, not Muhammad's.

Another instance of this is the *abd* in this verse: *So they found one of Our abds [abdan min ibadina] on whom We had bestowed a Mercy from Us, and We taught him knowledge from Our presence [ladunna]*, (18:66), where the *abd* is characterized as having knowledge not acquired by his own efforts, but as having knowledge directly and immediately bestowed on him by Allah.

So, now we have a situation where the act of *taharah* on this shoe/ foot discloses a radical ambiguity of existence. Now we come to *ijtihad*.[17]

> So, the *shar* is a *hukm* of Allah, not a *hukm* of the *aql* [intellect], as some of *them* believe. Therefore, the vision [r.'y.] of *taharah* of the shariah is based on Allah, One, Real. Because of this, it is not appropriate to contest the *hukm* of the *mujtahid*, as the *shar* [Law], which is a *hukm* of Allah, has

> already affirmed that *hukm* of the *mujtahid*: it is the *shar* of Allah to affirm whomever. This [*ijtihad*] is an issue in which all the experts of the schools of jurisprudence are falling into the forbidding, without calling to mind what we have pointed out, despite their knowing it. But they have been heedless of calling it to mind, so they have offended proper courtesy toward Allah in that, while the courteous among the worshippers of Allah succeed. So the one who faulted the *mujtahid* himself has in fact faulted the Real in what He affirmed as *hukm*.

The tearing of the shoe, which is outward, corresponds to the tearing of the shariah, which is also outward. Hence,

> If the *shar* is torn, it becomes *zahir* in some issue as one of the properties of unity which would remove a property of the *shar* completely, transferring the *hukm* to a *taharah* of that unity which is effecting a removal of a *hukm* of the shariah, just as one who relates all acts to Allah, from every perspective, does not concern himself with what becomes *zahir* as a consequence, whether contradictory or harmonious.

What is needed is purification from this problem; the shariah becomes torn and at some point ceases to be called shariah, as happens with torn shoes. But as long as the name 'shoe' does apply, wipe over the part which emerges. Ibn al-Arabi says,

> [T]hat is explicated, for that unity designated for this issue, is the perspective made *shar*, and this is that one say, *But Allah has created you and what you know*.[18] So the practices of the creation belong to Allah, despite the fact that they are related to us. But they are not related to Allah from every perspective, so they do not affect the wiping. The *hukm* about that would be as we have determined it.

In what preceded, the contours of Ibn al-Arabi's opposition to the use of *qiyas* (analogy)[19] also appear which we will consider briefly below. Simply stated, the interpretation and the application of the *shar* can never admit of purely human intervention, such as logic and analogy.

This is Ibn al-Arabi's discussion of *ijtihad*, and it is found even today. But one need not demand the entirety of this conception of *ijtihad* to still see a lively tradition of *ijtihad* in the face of the state of Islam. If we focus less on the state and the official proclamations of its ulema and more on the lived reality of Muslims, we see a different situation with *ijtihad*.

I. *Fiqh* and *Qada*

From one perspective of application of Law, the concept of there being closed gates of *ijtihad* is indeed odd. By relying on stultifying descriptions of a static legal discourse, Western scholars have missed the actual function of Islam in communities. A colleague recently asked me to go over his notes for a presentation on Islamic law. The enumeration of the 'sources of legal injunctions' (*usul al-ahkam*), or 'sources of legal discourse' (*usul al-fiqh*) was the conventional series of four: Quran, Sunna, scholarly consensus, and analogy (*qiyas*). The process of legal reasoning was the conventional one of searching the Quran for an explicit reading, then looking at the Sunna if there was nothing in the Quran, and then falling back on scholarly consensus, and if no consensus existed, then resorting to the extension of an explicit command by analogy.

This process is a methodology reached after the fact. In fact, the entire enterprise of the *usul al-fiqh* is highly contentious. As with most *post hoc* histories, it is difficult to re-evaluate the early history of the development of *fiqh* without the received version colouring our views. There was, and still is, no clear and obvious hierarchy in the first two sources. The Sunna gives stoning for adultery, the Quran whipping. The Quran makes circumambulation of the Kaaba merely permissible, the Sunna seems to make it obligatory. The Quran seems to have the feet wiped for *wudu*, as we shall see, but the Sunna is for washing. The list goes on: it is simply not obvious how the Quran and Sunna are to be taken, harmonized, or ranked. Adding the next two sources, consensus (*ijma*)—(whose consensus? when and where?)—and analogy, only adds to the confusion.

This *post hoc* method, tortuous in its implications, was obviously in dire need of personal interpretations, but the gates of *ijtihad* had been closed centuries before, so the hapless Muslim is constrained. I was startled to realize that the same description of the process of Islamic law which I had learned and absorbed years ago, after four years of direct study of the books of *fiqh*, simply looked bizarre.* But putting aside the received histories and the powerfully argued *al-Risalah* of the founding father Imam Shafii, and concentrating on the actual case by case debates, I was able to re-evaluate the history. It did take me a while to determine why that conventional description was so jarring: it is because the phenomenon being described is two-fold, but the description is one-sided. As Vogel pointed out, Western studies of Islam often omitted the law's application, possibly because of the linkages with the state of Islam and ulema, to the exclusion of the masses and unofficial, underground expressions of faith (such as Sufi shrine activity).

Islamic law has two sides. There is the *fiqh*, which is the superstructure of interpretation erected on the revealed text. This superstructure sorts and classifies the determinative properties (*ahkam*, singular *hukm*) of the revealed text into categories such as lawful/unlawful; obligatory, recommended, neutral, disliked, and forbidden; generally addressed and specifically addressed, abrogated and abrogating; and so on.

And then there is *qada*, the 'settling of affairs', as we saw described by Lawrence Rosen. The *fiqh* and *qada* are two separate activities.

Ijtihad is done everywhere and always, despite talk of its closed gates. The establishment of the *qiblah*, the direction of the Kaaba in Makkah, is a process of *ijtihad*, as the legal scholars always said. Accepting the *qiblah* of a particular mosque without personally assessing the *qiblah* on one's own is following another's authority (*taqlid*). Many mosques have an old architectural *qiblah* which those doing the *salah* today may ignore, turning instead in a direction perceived by *ijtihad* to be more truly the *qiblah*. In this example, the requirement to establish the *qiblah* is absolute: there is no room for *ijtihad* here to determine whether or not you must establish a *qiblah*. But the actual process of establishing the *qiblah* is *ijtihad*. Put these two together—the *fiqh* of the *qiblah* and the *qada* of determining it—and one can see why statements about there being no *ijtihad*, or a need for more, sound strange. There are two sides to Islamic law, and there are two types of *ijtihad*: there is the *ijtihad* of the *fiqh*, which has been severely restricted, and there is the *ijtihad* of the *qada*, which is constant in practice (at least in healthy communities).

This misunderstanding arises from not recognizing *fiqh* and *qada* as two different things and stems from not appreciating the concept of *hukm*, (a thing's property). The way to see how Islamic law operates is to focus on *hukm*. This word means property, with related meanings of ruling, decision, judgement. But the value of seeing *hukm* as property, and not as ruling or judgement is this: the divine name *hakim* is the 'one who establishes the property' of something;[20] and *Allah says al-haqq* (33;4), meaning the truth of a matter is what Allah says about it. So the key process of *fiqh* is understanding the *din*, religion, which recalls its Quranic derivation—*tafaqquh fil-din* (cf. 9:122)—and that is examining the entirety of novel things and issues and circumstances and assigning them their name,[21] which means giving things their *hukm*.

II. Naming

What the *qadi*, who Rosen describes, does is help disputants put names and properties on to their concerns. He is helping them to create a 'metasystem which creates order in a universe that is often experienced in a more disorderly way.'[22]

Knowledge in this scheme is knowing the *hukm* of a thing. And knowing the *hukm* first requires knowing names. In a preceding passage, Ibn al-Arabi said, 'And that only as long as it can be called a shoe—inevitably with this condition.' Shariah refrains run throughout the *Futuhat*, with Ibn al-Arabi always insisting on careful definition of names. As long as you have a shoe, the *taharah* of wiping over them is possible. Ibn al-Arabi does not propound the more stringent rules relating to tattered shoes—whether the holes involved are one or three inches wide, and so on.[23]

Ibn al-Arabi propounds the easiest position, which is as long as you can call the thing a shoe, it is possible to wipe it. When what is seen is not a shoe but tattered rags, for example, then the *hukm* of wiping it is no longer possible. The importance of names is described by Chodkiewicz in this way:

> In the *Futuhat*, Ibn al-Arabi casually recounts an anecdote that might conceivably serve as an exergue to the remarks that follow. The hero of the anecdote is Malik, the Imam founder of one of the four principal schools of Sunni jurisprudence.
>
> Malik b. Anas was asked: 'What is your opinion about the lawfulness of the flesh of the water pig [*khinzir al-ma*: an expression that refers to cetaceans in general, but dolphins in particular]?' He replied, '[*fa-afta*: a judicial consultation, not a simple exchange of words] that it was illegal'. An objection was made: 'Does this animal not belong to the family of marine animals [literally, 'fish', whose flesh is lawful]?' 'Certainly', he said, 'but you called it a pig [*khinzir*].'
>
> Some might be tempted to class this ambiguous cetacean among the taxonomic fantasies of a maniacal casuistry. But Ibn al-Arabi's mention of it on two different occasions shows it to be something completely different for him. What is in question here is the authority of the name [*hukm al-ism*] and the secret of naming [*tasmiya*], which leads us to the very heart of Ibn al-Arabi's hermeneutics.[24]

Most of the application of Law is getting definitions straight. As we saw above, the foundation of interpretation is language, and specifically the language of the Arab. Ironically enough, it is remarkable how liberating a literal reading of the textual tradition is. The *fiqh* approaches each issue with a thorough and exhaustive examination of every relevant piece of information. Was the command made specific for a particular audience, or a particular situation? Are there preconditions? What is the entire range of the key word in question? When did the command appear, and in what context? Debate and discussion fill pages upon pages for each detail. The liberating aspect is that the entire discursive system is designed to answer quite simply this question: What minimum does this command of Allah's require of us?[25]

As we saw, the *hakim* is the one who determines the *hukm* or property of a thing. Today in South and Southeast Asia, the word *hakim* is used for a traditional doctor. The word still retains its meaning, however, where the *hakim* as doctor seeks to determine the property of a person, to identify the constitution (*mizaj*) and to prescribe the medicine/food needed to restore the balance (*mizan*). That this is not a closed system is clear from the fact that historically, the *hakims* did not restrict themselves to the paucity of prophetic statements about explicitly health-related matters, described as 'Prophetic Medicine' (*tibb al-nabawi*), but instead incorporated Greek (*Yunani*) medicine into an Islamic discourse on health and disease.[26]

If we note that the word 'in-formation' may be glossed as 'data put in-formation', we can see how the *hakim* operates. The data is data, but the information is the way that data is filed and put into forms, and it is that process that is 'Islamic'.[27] So the important part is identifying novel things, (*hukm*); the central practice is taking new people with new problems and identifying the *hukm* over them and prescribing accordingly. Once the *hukm* is discovered, the remedy is indicated. Once the *qiblah* is determined, the direction one faces is indicated.

The reason then why the ulema (at least some of them) resisted the sultan and state is precisely because the state wants to seize the identification process by codifying and standardizing highly diverse human behaviour into narrowly defined and static categories. The *qadi* who insists that each case is unique, is not efficient, and the state can have none of that. The entire project of the ulema does not fit ideas of progress and efficiency which pervade typical development and social change paradigms.

Also, as opposed to a precedent- and adversarial- based legal system, fairness and justice are not seen as predictable outcomes based on repeatable events nor as the result of a dialectical process, but rather as the process of arriving at a unique description of a situation which restores a universe of harmony for the disputants, the *qadi*'s role being that of facilitator.

This is, too, a system which resists efficiency, as does the constant use of *shura* (consultation) for explicitly political affairs. No one could say that the Quaker or Amish systems of *shura* are efficient: but they are remarkably effective.[28]

Another indication that the project of the ulema resists centralization and state power is found in its rejection of 'one-man Islam' which involves a denigration of the slow, gradual, and cumulative nature of the ulema project and its substitution with a single perspective of reform that will solve all problems. Noah Ha Mim Keller, the translator of *Umdat al-Salik*, remarks that 'each school [of jurisprudence] does not merely comprise the work of a single Imam, but rather represents a large collectivity of scholars whose research in sacred Law and its ancillary disciplines has been characterized by considerable division of labour and specialization over a very long period of time . . . The result of this division of labour has been a body of legal texts that are arguably superior in evidence, detail, range, and in sheer usefulness to virtually any recent attempt to present Islam as a unified system of human life.'[29]

The basic methodology of Ibn al-Arabi and the non-state ulema stems from a concern with the literal, linguistic meaning of the text. Ibn al-Arabi goes further, being more literal and more keyed into linguistic possibilities than most of the ulema. Chodkiewicz notes Ibn al-Arabi's 'concern for considering each of God's words and silences', but understands that this 'is certainly not sufficient to convince his adversaries of his orthodoxy'. In fact, 'Nothing better illustrates the impossibility of satisfying the *ulama al-zahir* by rigorous fidelity to the *zahir* or Quranic text than the reading that Ibn al-Arabi does of the famous verse [42:11] *Laysa ka-mithlihi shay'un*.'[30] This verse, which means 'There is nothing which is H/his similar', has *ka* which must be explained. Chodkiewicz comments that Qushayri and al-Razi, among others, take the particle *ka* as *li-l-mubalagha* (having an intensifying function), something like, 'There is nothing at all which is *His* similar'.

But while Ibn al-Arabi takes this meaning throughout the *Futuhat*, he also reads another linguistic possibility of this verse. Chodkiewicz says, 'Ibn al-Arabi completes it by another one, which is its exact opposite. God does not speak to say nothing: the particle *ka* can thus also preserve all the force of its normal meaning. And the verse thus means: "There is nothing like His similar"—an interpretation that, for the *fuqaha*, is supremely blasphemous.'[31]

In his commentary on this verse (42:11), al-Razi affirms the 'problem' of accepting the Quran literally. He says, 'The *zahir* [obvious, literal] meaning of this verse has different modes; one says the intent of verse is to reject something similar to Allah, but the *zahir* requires the affirmation of something similar to Allah, because the *zahir* necessitates rejecting something similar to His similar, not something similar to Him.' Al-Razi, Ibn Hisham in *Mughni al-Labib*, and Ibn Aqil respond to this problem by citing the Arab usage of *ka* in the statement *ka-mithlika la yabkhulu*, that is, the likes of you would not be miserly, so we deny miserliness by your similar, and the Arab means denying miserliness by you, as al-Razi says it. Ibn Manzur sums up the problem by saying, *Laysa ka-mithlihi shay'un* means *laysa mithlahu*, and it could mean nothing but that, because if it is not said like that, this verse would affirm that He has a similar.

The ulema who promoted particular meanings of this verse did so for well-documented reasons. Al-Razi, for example, was concerned with the Jahmiyyah or Jabriyyah school of theology which over-abstracted divine attributes and tailored his argument to refute them. But the intellectual rigour of the ulema is such that ideas, even ideas the author is utterly opposed to, are presented straightforwardly. For example, in the long discussion of the issue of washing or wiping the feet during *wudu* presented by al-Razi, one could not discern which of the many arguments he presents would be approved of and which would be disapproved of, until he inserts his own comments directly onto the argument.

Another example of this is with the issue of a woman leading the *salah* when there are men present. There are arguments for and against. Abu Thawr, for example, takes the positive argument that the revealed text, 'Let him lead who is best at reciting [*aqra*] the Quran' is general, not specific to men. Ibn al-Arabi, as another example, takes the positive argument that leading a *salah* is *imamah* (leadership) and that *imamah* is a sub-set of being *kamal* (complete) (such that all complete people can be Imams, but not all Imams are complete), and since we know from an authentic *hadith* that among the complete people are Maryam and Asiyah (the wife of Pharoah), we know that *imamah* of women is permitted.

The only against argument proffered is that the Prophet (*sallallahu alayhi wa sallam)* is supposed to have said, 'Woman shall not lead man'. Now the majority of legal scholars through the ages have not accepted the *imamah* of women over men. When they argue, they generally leave aside the for arguments for this case. As for the against argument, scholars like al-Nawawi, Ibn Hajar, and al-Bayhaqi admit the *hadith*, 'Woman shall not lead men', is weak (and therefore cannot be used as evidence), but then say, 'But we [still] do not permit the *imamah* of woman over men'.

Added to the for arguments is the case of Umm Waraqah, who was commanded by the Prophet himself to be the Imam of her household in which there were men. Al-Darqutni, in an effort to divert this argument, goes to great lengths to fabricate a scenario where the men run out to the mosque before Umm Waraqah starts leading the prayer. Al-Bayhaqi tries to divert the argument by saying that the best rows for women are the back ones; this is a non-argument, because the woman may as well lead from the back rows or between the men's and the women's rows.

Ibn al-Arabi's acceptance of the position of those ulema who permit the woman leading men is based on the literal, outward, *fiqh* evidence. This is the basis of accepting one or another position. He is also able to delve into the inward or spiritual explanations for the outward truth. The inward affirmation of the outward position is found in crossing over from the outward to the inward. This he does by crossing over Man to *aql*[32] and Woman to *nafs*,[33] explaining that it is permissible for the *nafs* to lead the *aql* (but that is not permissible for *hawan*—caprice, which is crossed over to the *kafir*—to lead the *salah*). In this context, gender is inwardly determined; a female gender inwardly may exist in a male sex outwardly. More accurately, genders operate in a yin-yang mode.

One wonders what Muslim communities would look like if they took some of the positions held over the ages by the ulema, especially those not linked into state power. One can imagine far-reaching corrections and readjustments which could be made without extensive *ijtihad*.

III. Logic and Analogy

One of the ways in which positions such as this one, which forbids the leadership of women over men, gain sway, is by a storming of culture (paternalistic) over the legal text. The flexibility of opinion and cultural input into the legal discourse meant that the strict textual approach to *fiqh* and contextual approach to *qada* succumbed to sultanic forces. The kind of legal reasoning that emerges, then, seeks to cut off what Allah pronounced (*mantuq*) and fill in what Allah was silent about (*maskut*). In his strict rejection of all *qiyas* which is not explicitly *ijtihad*, Ibn al-Arabi recognizes the dangers of extending, through analogy, explicit commands into realms of silence. There is a firm boundary separating the *mantuq* and the *maskut*, and to breach the line is to take Lordship on oneself. To silence what was spoken and to vocalize what was silent is to assume Lordship. The *abd*, in complete contrast, seeks to be utterly passive and receptive to Allah's command, like the corpse in the washer's hands.

One of Iḅn al-Arabi's arguments against *qiyas* is found in his discussion of *tayammum* (preparing for *salah* by dusting the hands and face). To understand how *qiyas* is related to the issues surrounding *tayammum*, we need to understand how Ibn al-Arabi crosses over (cf. *itibar*) a *hukm* from the outwardness to the inwardness. The most felicitous folk, Ibn al-Arabi says, are those who follow the *hukm* of Allah in the outwardness and also in the inwardness. For Ibn al-Arabi, each *hukm* has an outer and one or more corresponding inner dimensions. First, the linguistic base. About *itibar* and *ibrah* (`b.r.), Ibn Manzur says, 'The *ibr* [crossing] of the arroyo.' And 'in the *hadith* of Abu Dharr there is, What were the *suhufu Musa* [books of Moses]? He said, They were all *ibarahs*. That is, they were like admonishments which people would heed and would put into practice.' Also 'in the *hadith* of Ibn Sirin, he said, I do [*itibar*] of *hadith*, the meaning of which is that he crosses over (`b.r.) the perspective of the *hadith* as he crosses it over with the Quran by its interpretation; for example, "the crow" is crossed over to the *fasiq* [bad man], and the rib to the woman, because the Prophet called the crow *fasiq* and declared the woman like the rib. The likes of that is done with allusions and nouns.' (The word *itibar* is the thing crossed over, in the Greek sense of metaphor.)

Ibn al-Arabi says,

> A *taharah* of sight for example, for the inwardness, is considering things through the eye of *itibar*, so one's eyes will not chase after distractions. The likes of this are not for any but the one who has realized the performance of the *taharah* set down by revelation in [different] places, each one of them. Allah said, *In this is an ibrah for the ones having sight* [3:13]. He made the *ibrah* with 'sight' because it is the secondary cause that leads to the inward, which is that to which the eye of insight crosses over. It is like this for each of the bodily parts.

Receptivity to divine speech *and* silence are necessary. This makes most kinds of analogical deduction, (*qiyas*) illegitimate.

One of Ibn al-Arabi's discussions about *qiyas* is found in his justification for taking the position that *tayammum* is not a substitute for purification. In this case of *tayammum*, the key properties in his discussion are water, dust, earth, knowledge, and *taqlid*. Water is crossed over to knowledge for those with insight, and if one examines the Quran, the water which animates dry earth and causes plants to grow is fluidly crossed over to knowledge which inspires the hard heart and causes good fruit to be produced. Dust and earth are humble, reminding the one with insight that we are dust to dust, and that the earth was made humble. Then, the *hukm* of *tayammum* is crossed over to situations where water—knowledge—is not found, or cannot be used.

For Ibn al-Arabi, *tayammum* is not a substitute for *wudu* or *ghusl*, as the ulema believe, but a *taharah* set down in the shariah in its own right. For Ibn al-Arabi, the only way to approach Allah in the *munajah* with Him,[34] which is the *salah*, is to do *taharah* with water or with dust. Because each is set down by the *shar* (Law-giver), there is no question of denigrating *taharah* with dust simply because dust is not a linguistic or rational form of purification.

Therefore, in the absence of knowledge, *taqlid* is required. For Ibn-al-Arabi *taqlid* is certainly not following the authority of one of the experts of opinion, but of one of the 'people of remembrance'[35] or *ahl dhikr*, which means the one who can tell the person without knowledge that this or that is indeed the *hukm* of Allah, or of His messenger. Ibn al-Arabi says this:

> Our position is that *tayammum* is not a substitute but rather a *taharah* set down by *shar*, specified and designated for a specific state; the One who revealed it revealed the use of water for this specified worship, and it is Allah, and his Messenger (*sallallahu alayhi wa sallam*), so it is not a substitute. Rather it is based on an extraction of the property for this issue, from a revealed text mentioned in the Book or Sunna, encompassing the property for this issue in a synopsis of that discourse. It is the *fiqh* of the *din*. He said, *Let a contingent from every expedition remain behind to apply themselves [cf. tafaqquh] to the din and admonish the people when they return to them-that thus they may learn to guard themselves[against evil]* {9:122}—and we do not need *qiyas* for that!

Taking a standard argument, that we have no revealed text regulating beating one's father with a stick, and that we need to extend the 'Say not *uff*[36] to them' (17:23) to cover beating with a stick, Ibn al-Arabi says this:

> We say that we do not have the exercise of declaring the property over the *shar* [Law-giver] concerning anything, even among the things it is permitted that we be responsible for—no declaring of the property, especially not in the likes of this. If there had not been mentioned explicitly in the revelation something other than this [saying of *uff*] *qiyas* would not have been made required of us, and we do not augment it by the saying of *uff*. Rather we make as *hukm* what He mentioned, and it is His statement, *treat with kindness*

> *your parents* [17:23]—so the address is undifferentiated; we extract from this synopsis the *hukm* about everything which is not a kindness. Beating with a stick is not one of the kindnesses which has been commanded by the revelation in our relationships with our parents. So we did not make as *hukm* anything but the revealed text, and we do not need *qiyas*.
>
> The *din* is perfected, and it is not permitted to add to it, just as subtracting from it is not permitted. So the one who beat his father with a stick has not treated him kindly, and the one who did not treat kindly his parents has rejected what Allah commanded of him, that he practise kindness toward his parents. And the one who opposed the word of his parents, and did what his parents do not approve of, something which is permissible for him to leave off, has in fact been disrespectful to them both. And it has been established that disrespect to parents is one of the great sins. Because of this, we argued that the *taharah* with dust—and it is *tayammum*—is not a substitute. Rather it is set down by *shar*, just as *taharah* with water was made *shar*.

Besides the peril one places oneself in with breaching boundaries between what Allah has stated explicitly and what He has not stated, between the *mantuq* and the *maskut*, societies yield to pressures to make Islam a culture. Thus, the patriarchy and racism found in culture is extended analogically to Islam.

The contest over *ijtihad* revolves around the role the intellect will play in determining rulings. For Ibn al-Arabi, *ijtihad* requires an *abd* who is so effaced that in effect the *hukm* discovered is the *hukm* of Allah. Novelty does not faze the *abd*, because in fact 'Every moment He is upon some task' (*kulla yawmin huwa fi shanin*, 55:29), nor the *qadi* who sees each case as novel and unique. Whether desire for standardization and codification is natural or state-induced, the fact remains that the complacency this produces is antithetical to the perpetual receptivity—even confusion—required by the radical ambiguity of existence.

Notes

1. Frank E. Vogel (1993). The Closing of the Door of *Ijtihad* and the Application of the Law. *American Journal of Islamic Social Sciences* 10,3:396.
2. Quoted in Vogel (1993).
3. This is the word *qada* which we saw was related to the 'one who settles the affairs', the *qadi*.
4. Vogel (1993).
5. Ibid.
6. Al-Sharani. *Mizan al-Kubra*.
7. *Subul al-Salam* (Indonesia: Maktubah wa Matbaah Taha).
8. Al-Sharani.
9. Vogel.
10. The number is chosen somewhat haphazardly; this was one of my counts from a standard *fiqh* book: depending on how one counts what will be an issue, a subject, and a subdivision, a certain number would be reached. Generally speaking, there are 200-300 issues in *ibadat* and the rest in *muamalat*. As far as I can determine, there is a standard corpus of some number of issues which all the Sunni works address.
11. In a review of William C. Chittick's *The Sufi Path of Knowledge*, Th. Emil Homerin (1992) *JAAR* comments that, 'When speaking of Islam prior to this century, whether in Morocco or Egypt, Turkey, Iran, or India, and, I suspect, in Malaysia and Indonesia too, it makes little sense to posit a normative Islam as distinct from—let alone as opposed to—Sufism. Very few of the ulema, or Muslims for that matter, were not Sufis in some very real sense of the term. Stated simply, Sufism was, and for many still is, a vital part of any normative Islam'.
12. Michael Sells' (1994) recent work *Mystical Languages of Unsaying* explores the mystical 'grammar' of these activities; my shorthand of lower-case and capital letters is merely to suggest the kind of activity going on here. I might add that language is a centring force of Islamic

civilization, whether in art (hence the importance of calligraphy) or devotion (for example, the positions of *salah* described as [*alif*], [*lam*], [*mim*]). The same kind of language games are important in rap, for instance, and among the Five Percenters (see Yusuf Nuruddin's article in Haddad and Smith, editors, *Muslims Communities in North America* 1994). Making language games about soles and souls is certainly parallel to the kind of activity that Sufis and scholars do. The only difference is that the Sufis and scholars ground their activity in the grammar, lexicography, and etiology of a language—the Arab language—which is privileged divinely as *hukman arabiyyan* and *quaranan arabiyyan*.

13. Muhammad Abul Fadl Ibrahim (ed.) (1958). *Diwan Imru-al-Qays* (Egypt). This and other passages from Ibn Manzur are from my 1995 translation *Mysteries of Purity* from his *Futuhat al-Makkiyyah*.
14. Among the ulema, there is a disagreement on this issue, with positions of wiping, washing, wiping or washing, washing and wiping, based on the linguistically complex interpretations of the *wudu* verse, found in 5:6 (*fa aghsilu-wa amsahu bi ruusikum was arjul-i/a/u-kum*); it is an issue occasioning intricate and voluminous debate, summarized in Chapter Five.
15. A perfect example of this *adab* is the behaviour of Khidr related in 18:79-82. When Khidr destroyed the boat in order to make it useless for the king who was seizing boats, he says, 'I wanted [*fa aradtu*] to do it.' Destruction of property is blameworthy, so Khidr takes the credit. When he killed the boy, he did so because the boy would grow up 'rebellious and ungrateful'. In exchange, the parents got a pure son. Khidr shifts to the first person plural, 'we', in describing this event. He says, 'We wanted [*fa aradna*] that Allah give them a better son.' Khidr is therefore credited with the killing, but the praiseworthy act of providing a better son is credited to Allah. As for the wall which was built up to hide a treasure until the two youths could claim it, building a wall is entirely praiseworthy, so both the act of building the wall and the intent of helping out the children is credited to the Lord. Khidr says, 'Your Lord wanted' [*fa arada rabbuka*].
16. William C. Chittick (1989). *The Sufi Path of Knowledge* (SUNY). This *hadith qudsi* is 'perhaps the most famous and most frequently quoted of all Divine Sayings among later Muslim writers', as Graham remarks, in William A. Graham (1977) *Divine Word and Prophetic*

Word in Early Islam (The Hague: Mouton). It is found in Sahih Bukhari 81:38:2 as, 'The messenger of Allah, Allah bless him and preserve him, said that Allah said, One who takes My *wali* as an enemy I declare war on him. My *abd* does not draw near Me with anything more dear to me than what I made required of him. My *abd* then continues to draw near Me with supererogatory prayers until I love him, and when I love him, I become the ear with which he hears, and his eye with which he sees, and his hand with which he grasps, and his foot with which he walks. If he asks Me, I give it to him. If he seeks My protection, I protect him. I do not hesitate to do something as I hesitate to take the soul of the believer who hates death, as I hate to harm him.'

17. The word *mujtahid* means one who does *ijtihad*. Ibn Manzur says, 'There is the *hadith* of Muadh, who said, *ajtahida* [I will do *ijtihad*] of my *ray* [vision, reflection], which means to do one's utmost in searching for the *amr* [command/matter],' which is next described as 'extending the book and Sunna [to novel situations].' Muadh was delegated by the messenger of Allah to be a judge. When asked how he would judge, he said he would judge according to the Book. And if the appropriate response is not there? Then the Sunna. And if it is not there? Then I will do *ijtihad* of my *ray*. Because the messenger of Allah affirmed this triad, *ijtihad* of *ray* became *shar*.
18. An allusion to the prophet Abraham's denunciation of his community's idol-worship: after striking the idols with his right hand he said, 'Do you worship that which you yourselves have carved? But Allah has created you and what you do' [cf. *amal*] [37:95-96].
19. About *qiyas*, Ibn Manzur says, '*qiyas* of something is to measure it against its like'.
20. For example, *dhalikum hukmu Llahi yahkumu baynakum wa Llahu alimun hakimun* (60:10) and *wa law la fadlu Llahi alaykum wa rahmutuhu wa anna Llaha tawwabun hakimun* (24:10).
21. Ibn al-Arabi and the traditional Sufi scholars conceive of 'novel situations' every moment, because *Every day He is upon some affair* (55:29).
22. Rosen (1989).
23. As with all issues of disagreement among the ulema, there are easier and more difficult or stringent positions; al-Sharani characterizes this spectrum as one end being more ponderous, and the other more light in the balance. Except for issues such as those surrounding reciting and touching the Quran, for example, Ibn al-Arabi generally chooses

and argues for the easier positions held by the ulema through the ages.

24. Michel Chodkiewicz (1993). *An Ocean Without Shore: Ibn Arabi, The Book, and the Law* (SUNY).
25. Unfortunately, we always have pronouncements, like that of the Imam of al-Azhar extolling female circumcision (about this subject see my article in *Women and Health* 23:1995) which are erroneous and deceiving; they ignore the Quran and Sunna and centuries of *fiqh* scholarship and research; worse, they arrogate prophethood and create their own religion.
26. Although there are isolated objections, the *hakim*s generally recognize that the *tibb al-nabawi* is insufficient to support an Islamic system of health, as Dr Jurnalis Uddin remarks in the *Journal Kedokteran YARSI* 1993. I had the opportunity in November 1993 to lecture at *YARSI* (Islamic Hospital Foundation, Indonesia) and converse with Dr Jurnalis Uddin, who is working to integrate Islamic concepts and modern medicine into a system of medical education and practice suited to Indonesia.
27. Albert Hourani refers to this process of articulating new bodies of knowledge in Islamic terms and formats. He says, 'even the *falsifa* [philosophy] must now be seen, not as Greek philosophers in Arab clothes, but as Muslims using the concepts and methods of Greek philosophy to give their own explanation of the Islamic faith', quoted in Edward Said (1981). *Covering Islam* (New York: Pantheon).
28. There is an interesting revisionist claim that the US Constitution borrowed thoroughly from the 'Iroquois Seven Nations' constitution, but omits, most glaringly, the concept of consultation for all matters, including attack by enemies. The weak Congressional War Powers Act could then be seen as an attempt to close barn doors continually stormed by the Executive.
29. *Reliance of the Traveller: A Classic Manual of Islamic Sacred Law*: Ahmad Ibn al-Naqib al-Misri's *Umdat al-Salik*, translated by Noah Ha Mim Keller (second printing 1993), (Sunna Books, P.O. Box 6143, Evanston, IL 60204).
30. Chodkiewicz.
31. Ibid.
32. Ibn al-Arabi generally uses this term in its original sense of binding and fettering, as he sees the 'intellect' as constricted and fettering, in contrast to the 'heart'. In this context *aql* might be glossed 'fettering rationally'.

33. In the first instance of this 'crossing over' (*itibar*) of *nafs* to Woman, Ibn al-Arabi cites, *I do call to witness the self-reproaching nafs* [75:2] and *O nafs al-mutma'innatu [come back to your Lord well-pleased, and he is well-pleased*] (89:27), calling attention to the fact that these usages are feminine. Ibn Manzur says, 'It is said in a commentary to His words *O nafs al-mutma'innatu* that is the one who has calmed down [t.m.n.] faith and humbled itself before its Lord.'
34. The concept of *munajah* is based on the *hadith qudsi* where Allah says, *I have divided the salah into two halves, between Me and My abd, and My abd shall have what he asks. When the abd says, al-hamdu li-Llah rabb al-alamin, Allah says, My abd has praised Me*, and so on throughout the opening chapter recited in every prayer cycle of the *salah*, recorded in Muslim, *Musnad*, Tirmidhi, *Muwatta*, Nasai, and Abu Dawud. William Graham (1977). *Divine World.*
35. This is based on the Quranic phrase, *fasalu ahl al-dhikr in kuntum la talamun*. The verse is, *We did not send before you any but human beings, to whom We gave inspiration: Ask the folk of dhikr if you do not know.* About this, al-Razi says: 'One, Ibn Abbas said this means the folk of the Torah, and *dhikr* means the Torah, and the proof of that is His statement; *We wrote in the Zubur [Psalms], after the dhikr, that My right worshippers shall inherit the earth* [21:105], meaning, in the Torah. Two, al-Zajjaj said the folk of *dhikr* are those who know the meanings of Allah's books, and they are the ones who know that all of the prophets were human beings. Three, the folk of *dhikr* are the folk of knowledge about past reports, as knowledge of something is recollecting [cf. *dhikr*] it.'

    Al-Razi then says, 'An argument for denying *qiyas* based on this verse goes this way: When there comes to one made responsible for something some new development, and he knows its property [*hukm*], *qiyas* is not permitted for him. If he does not know its property, obligatory on him is asking someone who knows its property. This is the obvious/literal meaning of the verse. But if *qiyas* were an argumentation, he would not have been obliged to ask the knower, because it would be possible to extract the property [of the new development] by means of *qiyas*, so it is established that permitting the validity of *qiyas* requires giving up the validity of the obvious/literal meaning of this verse, so it is therefore necessary that one not permit *qiyas*. Allah knows best. But the response to this is that permitting the validity of *qiyas* is based on the consensus of its experts, and consensus is stronger than this particular evidence [the literal meaning of the verse]. But Allah knows best.'

36. *Uff*: Ibn Manzur says, '*uff* is a word of annoyance.'

Chapter 4

Ibn al-Arabi's Legal Literalism

> Ibn Arabi is not specifically pointing to some outwardly 'reformable' defect in the teaching and transmission of the law in his time, nor to the fraudulent pretensions or normal defects of particular individuals. Rather he is primary alluding here to the fundamental—and in our present circumstances, humanly inescapable—problem that the just, appropriate application and interpretation of the traditional sources concerning the divine commands and their historical application by the Prophet usually require a far deeper understanding of both their ultimate contexts and intentions and the relevant factors in each particular case than can be expected of any but the rarest individuals, those whose every action is divinely inspired and protected from error. As he remarks, more openly in section II-7 below, those truly qualified 'authorities' (the true *wulat*) in any age, whether or not they outwardly rule, are none other than the divinely guided 'saints'—i.e., the *awliya* (a term drawn from the same Arabic root as the words translated as 'authority' in these passages, and having explicit connotations of spiritual authority [*wilaya*] that are not readily conveyed by the term 'saint' in Western languages). (James Winston Morris, in Michel Chodkiewicz (ed.) (1988). *Les Illuminations de La Mecque* (Paris: Sindbad).

Let us examine the methodological basis for Ibn al-Arabi's *fiqh*, and then two cases of that method in practice. Ibn al-Arabi describes his colleagues as *ummal*, those entrusted to act, among the ulema, those who know.[1] As with all the technical words used by Ibn al-Arabi, this finds sufficient description in the Arab language, which is not the growing and changing language of Arabic but the language of the Quran. Ibn Manzur says about the word *amil*, which is the singular of *ummal*, 'The *amil* is the one who is put in charge [w.l.y., cf. *wilayah* and *awliya*] of someone's affairs, his wealth, his property, and his works.' The actual self of the true *amil* is invisible, because the activity one sees is rather that of the one on whose behalf the *amil* negotiates or contracts or speaks. Hence the description of the 'people put in charge', the *awliya: When they are seen, Allah is remembered.*[2]

Another word describing people who give a certain kind of command is *umara* (*amr*, a.m.r.), where when 'they' command, 'He' commands. The superimposition of commands comes about with literal transmission. They are, Ibn al-Arabi says, *umara* who hear the divine Word and give it back just as they heard it, word by word. He says,

> This [reward] does not occur except to one who propagates the revelation from the Quran or Sunna with the words which it came in. And this does not happen except for the transmitters of the revelation, among the reciters and transmitters of *hadith*, and for the legal scholars; but not for the one who transmits the *hadith* according to meaning (that is, not literally), like Sufyan al-Thawri and others believed in doing.[3]

The problem with such transmission is that what is being transmitted is one's own understanding of a particular *hadith*. Such a transmitter has in fact falsely claimed to be a messenger himself. In great contrast, the *amil* transmits the word directly, without intervention and without adding his[4] own ideas or understandings. The ones who propagate the revelation as they heard it, and give back the message as they heard it, the reciters and transmitters of *hadith*, 'they will assemble at the row of the messengers, on them peace.'[5] Because it is easy to transmit literally and exactly, and because it is difficult to be a prophet and carry the burdens of caring for a community, Ibn al-Arabi links the *hadith*, *There will be a people on the day of judgement the prophets will be jealous of*,[6] to this situation.[7]

Thus the importance of literal transmission. Besides this literal transmission which allows one to assemble with the prophets, there is another prophet-like activity. That activity is *ijtihad*, which looks like the creation of Law, while we know and accept as a tenet that the creation of shariah ended with Muhammad. Given that the decision of the *mujtahid* (one who does *ijtihad*) is confirmed by the shariah, given that new law is impossible, and given that, *There is no messenger after me, nor prophet*, Ibn al-Arabi categorizes that act of the *mujtahid* as giving him the degree of the prophets but without giving them Law. He says,

> Allah honoured His messenger by making his people witnesses to the nations of prophets as He made the prophets witnesses to their nations. Then He made this nation special, meaning its ulema, by making Law for them *ijtihad* of the legal properties [*ahkam*, singular *hukm*], and by determining as the *hukm* what their *ijtihad* leads them to.[8]

Then,

> Such a one in this nation would not be a prophet, as he is not a prophet

through revelation sent down. But Allah made law for the ulema of this nation their *ijtihad*, just as He said to His Prophet, *So that you would judge*[9] [h.k.m.] *among the people by what Allah showed you* [4:105]; the *mujtahid* does not judge except by what Allah shows him in his *ijtihad*.[10]

One characteristic of *ijtihad* is that the right determination gets extra reward and the wrong determination still gets one reward. The standard text for this situation is found in *Subul al-Salam*, from Amr Ibn al-As, that 'He heard the messenger of Allah (*salla llahu alayhi was salaam*) saying, When the *hakim* [h.k.m.] determines the *hukm*, that is [interjects the author of *Subul al-Salam*], when he wants to determine the *hukm*, based on his word, let him do *ijtihad*, because *ijtihad* is done before the *hukm* [is determined], then if he hits the mark, he gets two rewards, and when he determines the *hukm* and does *ijtihad* and errs, that is, is not consistent with what the *hukm* is with Allah, then he gets one reward'.

There is also a lesser known *hadith*. In *Musnad* Ibn Hanbal 2:187, *haddathana* [it was told to us in the form of a *hadith* by] Abd-Allah *haddathani* [it was told to me in the form of a *hadith* by] my father [Ahmad ibn Hanbal] *haddathana* Hasan *haddathana* Ibn Lahiah *haddathana* Amr Ibn al-As who reported that he said, 'I heard [. . .] and the messenger of Allah came and he said, When the *qadi* judges [q.d.y.] and does *ijtihad*, and hits the mark, he has ten rewards; and when he does *ijtihad* and errs, he has one or two rewards.'

One of the ways Ibn al-Arabi explains this characteristic is found in his *fiqh* discussion of the prayer during the eclipse. He crosses over from the outward legal positions to the inward truths to show that if 'the *mujtahid* errs, he is at the level of the one who is in the concealed area of the eclipsed area. There is no burden on him; he is given one reward.'[11] But there are those who, in full daylight, still refuse the light. About them, he says,

> But if the revealed text appears to him, and he leaves it in favour of his own opinion [*ray*] of his *qiyas* [deduction], manifesting his false allegation, there is no excuse for him before Allah, and he has offended.[12]

Continuing, he says,

> Most of this comes about with the legal scholars following those who said to them, 'Do not follow us blindly, but follow the *hadith* which comes to you, if it opposes what we have determined as *hukm* [legal property], because the *hadith* is our *madhhab* [way, school]. We do not determine anything except by the evidence which appears to us, and which appears to us to be evidence;

> we do not make requisite anything other than that. We have not made requisite on you all following us, but we have made requisite on you to be petitioners of us.'[13]

These eclipsed legal scholars refuse the text itself. They do not appreciate that as the moment changes, the situation changes, and the legal properties change accordingly. Ibn al-Arabi says,

> During every moment, during a single event, the *hukm* [legal property] alters according to the *mujtahid*. Because of this, [Imam] Malik used to say, when someone asked him [for a legal decision] about an event, 'Did it occur?' If he said, 'No', he would say 'I will not give a *fatwa* [legal opinion].' If he said, 'Yes', he would give a *fatwa* at that moment according to what his evidence gave him. The blind follower [q.l.d.] of the legal scholars of our times has decided that he has fulfilled the duty of his following his leader by following the *hadith* which his Imam commanded him, and his blind following of the *hukm*, despite finding something which opposes. So he disobeys Allah, in His word, *So take what the messenger gives you, and adhere to it* [59:7], and he disobeys the messenger, in his word, *So obey him*, because he [Muhammad] did not say anything except from a command of his Lord. And he disobeys his Imam,[14] in his word, 'Take the *hadith* when it is sent to you, and scorn my word.'[15]

They 'are in eclipse perpetually, endless for them until the day of judgement. They are not with Allah, nor are they with His messenger, nor with their Imam. Of them Allah and His messenger and their Imams have washed their hands and they have no proof in respect to Allah. So let them see who gathers with these!'[16]

I. First Case

Respect for the literal words and phrases of the revelation involves respect for the silences as well. Ibn al-Arabi condemns the silences of the revelation being filled in with arrogant noise, often justified as *qiyas* (analogical deduction). There are two kinds of *mujtahids*, he says at one point. One predominates declaring taboo and the other predominates lifting difficulties (where the word is *haraj*, about which Ibn Manzur says, 'You are in *haraj*, that is, in tightness and constriction', and based on the verse, *We did not make any haraj on you all in the religion* [22:28], by *adhering to the verses and by returning to the root* [*asl*].[17] The latter 'is according to Allah closer to Allah and greater in level than the one who predominates declaring taboo, as taboo is an accidental thing which occurs randomly on the *asl*.'

Given this, in the absence of taboo declared by the revealed text, one should return to the root. The first issue is about purification for the circumambulation of the Kaaba.[18] Ibn al-Arabi's position is, 'The circumambulation is permitted without *wudu* [a form of purification] for the man and the woman, unless the woman is a menstruant, based on the mention of the revealed text about it.'[19] The restriction is only on the menstruant, 'and not every worship makes as a precondition for it this outward purification [of *wudu*].' So, in the absence of a text for non-menstruants, men and women, Ibn al-Arabi's position is to return to the root; then, we find that everything in existence has a face towards Allah, and in this respect, it is pure.

> There is not in existence, according to the real determination, anything but The Pure, because the name *al-quddus* [The Holy] is associated with existence, and this is confirmed by His statement, 'To Him returns the entirety of the affair, so worship Him and rely on Him; your Lord is not Unaware of what you are doing' [11:123].[20]

Here, Ibn al-Arabi glosses the Quranic phrase 'what you are doing'. He says it refers to 'your interference between Allah and His creatures'. The word he uses, *tafriq* (f.r.q.), carries negative connotations, where Ibn Manzur says, *farraqa* (differentiation) for something good is *farq* (difference), and *farraqa* for something bad is *tafriq* (interference). Therefore, Ibn al-Arabi says, 'It is not appropriate to intervene between the creature and his Master except to enter in between the creature and the Master for good [*khayr*].' The negative intervention he is talking about is our speaking unfavourably about creation; the only proper intervention is interference for the good. He tells the following anecdote to demonstrate this. Ibn al-Arabi says,

> I met one of the Itinerants on the seashore, between Murcia and Manarah [in Tunis], and he said to me, I met in this place some one of the Truthful Substitutes when he was walking along the edge of the ocean; I greeted him and he returned the greeting. In the country was a great oppressive tyrant. I said to him, O you, have you seen what oppression there is in the country? He looked at me very angrily, and said to me: Do not say anything but the Good.[21]

Ibn al-Arabi explains, 'Because of this, Allah has made intercession Law and accepts legal excuses'. This is then linked to impurity. 'Impurity is an accidental thing, designated with Law-property; but purity is an essential thing'. Therefore, if there is an accidental property which emerges at some moment, then every other moment remains in its root property, which is purity.

Unfortunately, 'the legal scholars have been heedless of this, flailing at it, but they do not get it. We have already explained that one does not get into a disobedience completely, if one is a believer'.[22] Ibn al-Arabi explains that the situation of the believer who does something bad is described as, *One who mixed a wholesome act with another which was bad* [9:102]. The bad is the bad but the wholesome act is the faith of the believer (the *iman* of the *mumin*), because there is no disobedience by the believer except faith that accompanies it, which tells the believer that it is something disobedient. Hence, the 'faith which knows it is a disobedience is actually an obedience to Allah'.[23]

This conclusion combines with Ibn al-Arabi's *fiqh* position on praying behind a bad-doing leader, which focuses on the standard legal question which is based on the paradigmatic case of the Muslims praying behind al-Hajjaj and whether their prayers would be accepted. Ibn al-Arabi says that of course one cannot pray behind a bad-doing leader; but let us look at the legal facts. When al-Hajjaj does *wudu* for the *salah* and follows every condition for the validity of the *salah*, how can the name 'bad-doer' apply at that moment? Furthermore, 'al-Hajjaj and others in the context of their bad-doing are believers obeying their faith' that what bad they are doing is disobedience.[24]

Ibn al-Arabi sums up the situation as follows.

> The most amazing thing about this issue is that we are commanded to have a fine impression of people, forbidden to have a bad impression of people. We saw one whom we knew to be a bad-doer, who did *wudu*, and did the *salah*, so how could we apply to him the name of bad-doer during the moment of his worship? And how much more is the fine impression than the bad impression of him in doing it? We have no knowledge of the future for him, and we do not see what Allah did in the past with him, and the *hukm* [determinative property] belongs to the *waqt* [moment] of obedience which he is upon, being involved [right then] in obedience. So the fine impression is prior.[25]

Then, Ibn al-Arabi tells a story which is a warning to smug piety. He mentioned that someone 'firm in his religion told me about a man who was a legal scholar and a theologian who was a profligate of *nafs* [self].' This is a clue to the audience that this man struggled with his self (cf. *mujahidah*), and it is the terms of the struggle, not the discreet outcomes, which is of significance.

> He said to me, 'I came upon him in a gathering where wine was being circulated, and he was drinking with the rest. The drink was finished, and it was said to him, "Send someone to fetch us some drink". He said to them, "I shall not to do it! I have not decided upon disobedience completely. For me between the cups there is a turning for forgiveness, and I do not wait for the next cup, so when the cup gets in my hands, I wait and ask whether my Lord will give me success and I will leave it, or He will desert me and I will drink it".' Like this are the ulema, may Allah have mercy on them! This knowledgeable man died while there was in his heart a disappointment that he did not meet me, but he did meet me, but he did not recognize me, and he asked me about myself, and he had love for me, may Allah have mercy on him. That was in Murcia in the year 585.[26]

Concluding this section, Ibn al-Arabi tells another anecdote about a 'spiritual encounter' he had. He says,

> I witnessed the Real in my innermost being during a *waqiah* [spiritual encounter], and He said to me, 'Tell My worshippers what I designated as My generosity to the believer: the good rewarded with ten like it up to seven hundred as many, and the bad with only one like it. The bad act does not oppose faith in its being a bad act. So why would My worshipper despair of My mercy? *My mercy pervades everything* [7:156], and *I am according to the impression of My worshipper of Me, so let the impression of Me be Good*!'[27]

II. Second Case

The particular spiritual position of the believer presents certain legal, *fiqh* consequences. One of them is examined in the issue of praying over a person who has committed suicide. 'Should the one who killed himself be prayed over or not? There is one who said he should be prayed over, and there is one who said he should not be prayed over. For the first I argue.'[28]

To support this position, Ibn al-Arabi addresses the background situation of intercession. As usual, he finishes his enumeration of the ulema's outward legal positions with their inward complement, which he calls *itibar*, a crossover. He says here, 'A crossover for this section is that as Allah has permitted intercession in the *salah* over the dead, we know that Allah approves of that, and that the petition for him is accepted.' But we have the seemingly obvious *hadith* which at first glance seems to refute that background. It is reported that *The one who kills himself abides in the fire, abiding therein ever,*[29] and that *The Garden is forbidden him.* People take that to mean that *salah* over the suicide should not be done, but Ibn al-Arabi works from another text which will challenge that first glance understanding.

One key text precedes the text above and has the phrase, *My worshipper rushes to me on his own*, where 'rushes', Ibn al-Arabi says, is an allusion to other texts, which are always taken positively. He says, 'The wisdom alluded to, here in this issue, is the word of Allah, *My worshipper [abd] rushes to Me by himself; I forbid him the Garden.* There is an allusion here and a reality, and the allusion is to *They race* [to the Good, 3:114] and *They are foremost* [in seeking forgiveness, 57:21] and *Who approaches Me an inch, I approach him a yard*[30]—all positive images. The root word 'rushes' includes the concept of taking one's own initiative. This contrasts with the usual situation, where Allah 'makes for him a specific limit [of lifespan]. But [the suicide] tries to hasten the meeting and *rushes* to Him before having come to that limit'. Now, this entire text, with rushing and with being forbidden the Garden, is in a differentiated mode (*tafsil*), and for that reason, it is possible—in the *fiqh* sense—to return to the undifferentiated mode, which is the root, the *asl* or *usul* (plural, roots). It can, he says, 'be brought toward the face which is best for the believer, for helping him out, with the *usul*,' and that 'is a priority'.[31]

When the text is differentiated, that is, made specific and detailed, such as, 'As for His statement about the one who killed himself by iron, or poison, or throwing himself from a mountain', then one can argue that,

> [I]t is not said in the *hadith* whether they are believers or something else [and this leaves the way open for debate], so one may advance a likelihood; and if the likely is going to be introduced, we return to the *usul* [basic, general, undifferentiated] texts, where we see that faith has dominion of power which, because of it, the ever-abiding without end in the fire is not possible. So we know, certainly, that the revelation must be reporting that about those who associate partners with Allah [*mushriks*], is designated that they will be punished forever, so he said, *Who kills himself with iron, among the mushriks, his iron in his hand will take him to the innermost fire of Jahannam, everlastingly, abiding therein everlastingly.* That is, this type of punishment is his determination in the fire. Like that, *Who drinks poison, and kills himself, sips it in the fire of Jahannam everlastingly, abiding therein everlastingly*, that is, that is the kind of punishment he is punished with, this *kafir* [ingrate]. And it is reported that *Who kills himself with something is punished with it.*[32]

Now, since we know that the believer's faith cannot be ultimately opposed, so we know that the text above must apply to the *mushrik*, 'even if the revelation did not specify, in this report, the sort [of person] itself, yet because the shariah proofs are taken from many different perspectives, one of them coming together with another, in order to strengthen one by another, as *the believer is to the believers like the brick wall*,[33] so one strengthens another.'

Also differentiated is the vision of the divine. We know that 'the folk of the Garden see their Lord with a blessed vision, after they have entered the garden, as the report says about the calling to the garden—*When the people take their places in the Garden they are called to a vision.*'

Ibn al-Arabi is going to separate the two events, the taking of their places in the Garden and their being called to a vision. He argues, then that it is possible that,

> Allah has specified that, for this one who rushes to Him himself by killing himself, His word *I have forbidden him the Garden* may be before meeting Him; the blessed vision preceded the suicide meeting of Allah, and *then* he would enter the Garden, because the suicide saw that Allah was more merciful than the situation he was in, the circumstances which were the cause for him of this rushing. Otherwise, he would not have imagined that the repose with Allah would be better than the punishment which he was in when he rushes *to Him*.

To back up this argument, Ibn al-Arabi recalls the *hadith* we just saw: *I am according to the impression of My worshipper of Me; so let the impression of Me be Good.*

> Allah says, *ana inda zann abdi bi, fa-l-yazunna bi khayr* [*I am according to the impression of My worshipper of Me; so let the impression of Me be Good*], and the suicide, if he is a believer, has a Good impression of his Lord. It was the Good impression of his Lord that made him kill himself. This is more suitable, that one attribute to him the phrasing of this divine report. Well, there is no revealed text which clearly states a contradiction to this *tawil* [interpretation], even if it seems far-fetched; may the observer in his observation keep far away from the stipulated roots which would contradict this *tawil* with eternal wretchedness [for him]! So if he is present in it and balances it, he will recognize what we say about it. In the authentic report, there is *They will exit who have in their hearts the least, least of a grain of mustard of faith*, and nothing else remains except what we said about it. Allah did not say in this report anything but that he *forbade him the Garden*, only.

In effect, it is the job of the legal scholar (the observer above) to argue the best possible case, in this case, for the suicide. Ibn al-Arabi admits that his interpretation is far-fetched, but the argument is nevertheless logical and complies with the technical rules of the *fiqh*.

> So if we argue—for the chastisement, then the Garden is something forbidden to him that he enter without chastisement, like with the person of great sins. The report is a text for the suicide and others, among the people of great sins—they are upon the *hukm* [property] of [divine] volition, because *the man written down in the scrolls will not enter the fire*, even though he is one of the ones of great sins, if there was nothing with him but *la ilaha* in all his Islam in his period of life in the world.[34]
>
> The reason for the [extreme threat] is so that one would realize that the carrying out of the threat against the suicide is for before entering into the Garden, that he will not be forgiven suicide. But Allah is more Generous than that the carrying out the threat be imputed to Him; rather imputed to Him should be His volition and the preponderance of Generosity. It is as one of the Arabs (desert Arabs) described it:
>
> *inna idha awad-tu-hu (IV) aw wa d-tu-hu (I)*
> *la-akhlifu iadi*
> *wa unjizu mawidi*
> When I vow or swear
> I may go against my threat
> But I would carry out my promise.
>
> There is no mention in the revealed text about the threat [*iad*, root w.d.], but there is a mention about the promise [*wad* w.d.]: *Never think that Allah would go against His promise* [*to His messengers*] [14:47]. The *iad* is specifically used for bad [e.g., a threat], but *wad* may be either good or bad.

This argument is entirely justified linguistically.[35] Ibn Manzur says about the root w.d.,

> Al-Azhari said, In the *Arab* discourse, *wad-tu* [I promised] the man good, and *wada-tu* (I threatened) him bad. If they do not want to mention good, they say, *wad-tu* and do not insert the *a*, and when they do not want to mention bad, they say, *awad-tu* and do not omit the *a*. There is a verse from Amir ibn Tufayl:
>
> *inna in awad-tu-hu aw wad-tu-hu*
> *la-akhlifu iadi*
> *was unjizu mawidi.*

There are many who may object to Ibn al-Arabi's legal discourse, but it is not because he is not literal or firmly grounded in the revealed texts or does not follow the rules of legal discourse. But instead there seems to be another reason. Ibn al-Arabi's extreme literalism in the first case served to restore the essential quality of creation—purity. In the second case, he pushed literalism to the extreme and forced interpretations which he admitted were far-fetched. Why? To intercede positively for the eternal soul of a believer. We have quite the opposite legal discourse (if one can even use this term) today: a number of Islamicists who will identify impurity and pollution as essential and general traits of creation. Far-fetched interpretations are used to serve that purpose, but none are profferred to help out the believers.

That such a situation is perennial is suggested by Ibn al-Arabi's discussion of the addition during the prayer call of the morning *salah*, 'The *salah* is better than sleeping!' Some legal scholars argued that it was something introduced by Umar, so it is not strictly speaking Sunna (normative prophetic practice). But Ibn al-Arabi says, 'as for our position, we ourselves argue for it as being shariah, even though it is an act of Umar, because the revelation determined it in his word, *Who practises a practice [Sunna] which is fine, [and it is practised after him, he gets its reward and the like of the reward of theirs, without diminishing their rewards at all]*,[36] and we have no doubt that it is a fine Sunna [practice], so it is appropriate to express it as the shariah'. And then, 'Anyone who dislikes it, dislikes it only from fanaticism [*taassub*]. Who argues that, does not to do justice to it. We take refuge in Allah from the havoc of the egos!'[37]

Notes

1. From Uthman Yahya's critical edition of the *Futuhat*.
2. Ibn al-Arabi says, 'More than one has related to me, from one who related it, that the Prophet (*sallallahu alayhi wa sallam*) informed him that he was asked, O messenger of Allah, who are the *awliya* of Allah? The messenger of Allah (*sallallahu alayhi wa sallam*) replied, *Those who, when they are seen, Allah is remembered.* Hafiz Abu Nuaym mentioned it in his book *al-Hilyat* [*al-awliya*]. (See my *Mysteries of Purity*). In the *Sunan* of Ibn Majah, *zuhd, hadith* number 4119, we find '*haddathana* [it was told to us in the form of a *hadith*] Suwayd ibn Said *haddathana* Yahya ibn Sulaym from Ibn Khuthaym from Shahr ibn Hawshab from Asma binti Yazid that she heard RasuluLlah (*sallallahu alayhi wa sallam*) saying . . . *The best of you are the ones who, when they are seen, Allah is remembered.*'
3. *Futuhat.*
4. My use of the male pronoun parallels the Arab usage, which was truly inclusive. What happened after the formative period of the Arab language, where, for example, Aishah was called a man of vision (see the *Lisan, rajulah al-ray*), is well known. To take only one development, that of the Urdu language, in Urdu, the word *awrah*, which means the two private, shameful parts of the body, becomes divorced from males, attached to females, to mean woman—*aurat*, the shameful thing.
5. *Futuhat.*
6. The *musnad* records *hadith* number 2269, volume 8 (Dar al-Fikr edition 1991), from Abi Malik al-Ashari, that RasuluLlah (*sallallahu alyhi wa sallam*) said, 'O people, hear, understand, and know that Allah has worshippers neither prophets nor martyrs whom the prophets and martyrs will be jealous of over their seating places and their proximity to Allah.' Later in the *hadith* they are identified as follows: 'They are the *awliya* of Allah, the ones who have no fear nor sadness.'

7. Ibid.
8. Ibid.
9. The word h.k.m. only may be translated by 'judge' in the sense in English of using one's judgement, or someone having a good sense of judgement, that is, where judging means weighing, balancing, and evaluating multiple possibilities.
10. *Futuhat.*
11. Ibid.
12. Ibid.
13. Ibid.
14. That is, pre-eminent legal scholar, such as the four Imams—Malik, Shafii, Ahmad, and Abu Hanifah.
15. Ibid.
16. Ibid.
17. Ibid.
18. Ibid.
19. Ibid.
20. Ibid.
21. Ibid.
22. *Futuhat.* One of these discussions is found in *Mysteries of Purity* in the section on 'What happens to faith during disobedience?'
23. Ibid.
24. Ibid.
25. Ibid.
26. Ibid.
27. Ibid.
28. Ibid.
29. See *Sunan* al-Nasai, *al-janaiz*, '*man qatala nafsahu.*'
30. See *Musnad* Ibn Hanbal, *hadith* number 10228, from Abu Hurayrah, from the Prophet, that he said, 'Allah said, My *abd* is upon his impression of Me and I am with him when he calls Me; if he calls Me in his self, I call him in My self; if he calls Me in a gathering, I call him in a better and more pleasant gathering. If he approaches Me a hand span, I approach him an arm span, and if he approaches me an arm span, I approach him an outstretched span. If he comes to me strolling, I come to him hastening.'
31. This *fiqh* principle may be called '*add al-mumin min al-usul*'.
32. See *Sunan* al-Nasai, *iman*, '*al-hilf bi-millah siwa al-Islam*'.
33. See *Sunan* Ibn Majah, *zakah*, 'ajr al-khazin'.
34. Cf. *Sunan* Ibn Majah, *zuhd*, chapter 35, *hadith* number 4300.

35. The confluence of Ibn al-Arabi's ideas and the Arabi language (no coincidence in the names) is such that a colleague calls it the *arabi madhhab*, meaning both the school of Ibn al-Arabi and the positions based on the language.
36. *Sunan* Ibn Majah, *muqaddimah*, chapter 14, *hadith* number 207.
37. *Futuhat*.

CHAPTER 5

The Polysemantic Quran

Many Muslims, as they become educated, worldly-wise, or spiritual, assume that they will need to begin to approach and refer to the revelation symbolically and abstractly. They begin to look for ways to pull out deep or symbolic truths. If they have heard of Muhyi al-Din Ibn al-Arabi, they assume that he will be helpful because he is, as Henry Corbin constructed him, an expert of *tawil*, which means bringing something back to its origins (cf. *awwal*), as in allegorical interpretation. If they are fortunate, however, they will first or eventually find books or articles by James Winston Morris, Michel Chodkiewicz, or William Chittick, such as Chittick's *Sufi Path of Knowledge*, that demonstrate that Ibn al-Arabi uses the phrase *tawil* very rarely, and almost always pejoratively, and that he advocated strict orthopraxy.

What is the consequence of abstracting the text and treating it symbolically? My impression is that such an interpretative approach either becomes trivializing or fascist. The trivializing aspect comes about because truths are abstracted from their context and end up being recorded as bland statements, like 'Islam is peace', or 'Islam teaches us to be just', or 'Jihad means to struggle for peace'. In such a context, how important could careful adherence to the *ahkam* (legal properties) be? The fascist part comes about because the key interpreter gets to play games with symbols that are manipulated exclusively by him and his cohorts. In that context, external or outward or literal Islam, with its laws and regulations, is so much drivel for people not sufficiently elevated. (One could call the first approach *ibahiyyah* and the second *batiniyyah*).

In contrast, the consequence of closer readings of the revelation, of more grammatically aware and precise readings, of increased attention to the tiniest details of the revelation in its original language is, ironically, a discovery of a polysemantic and multifaceted text. The broadest, most varied and dynamic, vibrant and living understanding of the revelation comes from the closest, most careful, detailed, linguistic, and literally based reading. It happens too that the closest fidelity to the *ahkam* (such as those related to placing one's hands while standing during the *salah*, for example) opens up a range of authentic and true positions. Instead of denigrating the truth of following normative practices by trivializing them, this interpretation invests great significance and relevance to multiple true positions; instead of in-group fascism, this interpretation affirms other true positions, without denying any one of them.

In one passage we saw Ibn al-Arabi incorporating the peculiar linguistic fact that in the Arab language the word *khafiya* is its own antonym, such that, for those of the perception, the Hidden is the Manifest, the exposed is the concealed. When I mentioned this to a colleague of mine, she said that the secrets of the Quran are safely hidden away—in the outside, literal text! As with Poe's purloined letter, the best place to hide something is in the most exposed place. The *haqqiqah* is the shariah.

Let us examine the depths, details, and particularities of one portion of a verse to show what kind of polysemanticism comes about with a close, literal reading of the revelation. This portion of a verse in the chapter *al-Maidah* sets down the description of *wudu*. The portion reads, *O you who believe. When you go to the salah, wash your faces and your hands to the elbows and wipe your heads and your feet to the ankles* [5:6]. The two operative imperatives are wash (gh.s.l) and wipe (m.s.h.). The question is which imperative governs the phrase 'your feet'.

Wiping is where wet hands brush over the bodily part in question, whether head or foot. Wiping the feet entails a brisk movement similar to the wiping over the shoes, and Sunni scholars have generally believed this movement of wiping over the bare feet to be negated by the *hadith* evidence in which the Prophet Muhammad admonished a group of Muslims to pay attention to their heels in *wudu*, saying, 'Woe to the heels in hell-fire'.[1]

This particular line of argument unfolds as follows. The obvious and literal meaning of the verse in the Quranic Arabic indicates the feet, much as in English 'wipe your heads, and your feet', means 'wipe your heads, and wipe your feet'. But the *hadith* seems to indicate 'washing' the feet, so as to make sure the heels are covered in *wudu*. How should these two different indications be reconciled? We examine some of the major arguments which seek to do just that below, and then we examine Ibn al-Arabi's treatment of this issue.

Let us look first at three areas essential to this *fiqh* debate. First, the recitations involved for the verse; that is, the authentic, correct (*sahih*) recitations of the word 'your feet'. Second, the list of authorities and what method of *wudu* of the feet they practised, and why. Third, the arguments proffered by scholars over the ages to address this issue. The raw citations and data are to give the reader a glimpse of the intricacies and fine points of the classical scholarly discourse, where the direction one moves toward truth is not out towards abstraction and generalization, but in towards detail and specificity. As with fractal geometries, Escher's drawings, Borges and Eco's writings, the 'truth' of things lies in the patterns one perceives as one peers closely and with a narrower field of view. The weight of this massive debate should demonstrate the futility of the desire for conclusion and answers, and should begin to show us instead the value of searching for polysemanticism in randomness, complexities, and ambiguities.

I. Recitations

There are three recitations of 'your feet', namely *arjulakum*[2] (with *nasb*), *arjulikum* (with *khafd*), and *arjulukum* (with *raf*).

1.1 The first recitation is recited by Nafi ibn Abu Nuaym (169/785), Asim ibn Abu al-Nujud (127/744), and Ali ibn Hamzah al-Kasai (189/801).
1.2 The second recitation of *arjulikum* with *khafd* is that of Abd-Allah Ibn Kathir (120/737), Abu Amr ibn al-Ala (1455/771), and Hamzah ibn Habib (156/772).
1.3 For the third recitation, Nafi is reported, by Walid ibn Muslim, to have also recited *arjulukum* with *raf*, and it is the recitation of Hasan and al-Amash Sulayman.[3]

Generally, but not necessarily, as we shall see, the recitation of *arjulakum* supports a reading that implies that the operative imperative here is 'wash'; the recitation of *arjulikum* supports a reading that implies that the operative imperative is the proximate verb 'wipe'; and the rare recitation *arjulukum* supports a reading that implies that either of the two imperatives are operative—*wipe and wash* your feet.

II. Authorities

The following are authoritative positions of early Muslims.

i. *Arjulakum* : Washing

Urwah ibn Zubair *(nasb)*: recorded in Ibn Mundhir.[4]

Mujahid ibn Jabr *(nasb)*: in Ibn Mundhir.

Nafi ibn Abd al-Rahman *(nasb)*: reported from Abu Ubayd, in Ibn Mundhir.

Kisai *(nasb)*: in Ibn Mundhir.

Abu Ubayd al-Qassim ibn Salam *(nasb)*: in Ibn Mundhir.

Al-Shafii *(nasb)*: in Ibn Mundhir.

Ali *(nasb)*: al-Qurtubi records, 'Asim ibn Kalib reported from Abd al-Rahman that he said, Hasan and Hussayn, Allah's mercy on them, recited *wa arjulikum*, and Ali heard that, and was adjudicating between the people, and said *arjulakum*.' Ibn Mundhir confirms that Ali recited with *nasb*.

ii. *Arjulakum* : Wiping

Ibn Masud *: (nasb :* wiping*);*

Ibn Abbas *(nasb :* wiping*)*: al-Qurtubi records, 'It was reported from Ibn Abbas that he said *wudu* is two washings [arms and face] and two wipings [head and feet]'. Ibn Qudamah records, 'It is related from Ibn Abbas that he said, I do not find in the Book of Allah anything but two washings and two wipings.'[5]

Ibn Kathir records that Ibn Abbas wiped the feet. He says, 'Ibn Abu Hatim said, *haddathana* my father *haddathana* Abu Mamar al-Munqari *haddathana* Abd al-Wahhab *Haddathana* Ali ibn Zayd from Yusuf ibn Mahran from Ibn Abbas about this verse that it is a wiping.'[6]

Ibn Majah records in his *Sunan, 'haddathana* Abu Bakr ibn Abi Shaybah *haddathana* Ibn Ulayyah, from Ruhi ibn al-Qasim from Abd-Allah ibn Muhammad ibn Aqil from Rubayya, who said, Ibn Abbas came to me and he asked me about this *hadith*, that is, the *hadith* in which it was mentioned that the messenger of Allah (*sallallahu alayhi wa sallam*) did *wudu* and washed his feet. Ibn Abbas said, "The people insist on nothing but washing, but I do not find in the Book of Allah anything but wiping".'[7]

iii. *Arjulikum* : Wiping

Al-Hasan al-Basri : in Ibn Mundhir.

Sulayman ibn Mahran al-Amash : in Ibn Mundhir.

Abu Jafar : al-Razi records, 'The people disagree about wiping the feet and washing them', and Ibn Abbas, Anas ibn Malik, Ikrimah, Shubi, and Abu Jafar Muhammad ibn Ali obligate wiping, and it is the position of the Imamiyyah among the Shiah.'

Ikrimah ibn Abd-Allah: al-Qurtubi records, 'Ikrimah used to wipe his feet. He said there is no washing for the feet: The Quran was sent down with wiping them.' He also records that Ibn Jarir said, '*haddathana* Yaqub *haddathana* Ibn Uliyah *haddathana* Ayub who said, "I saw Ikrimah wiping his feet, and he argued for it".'

Abu Dharr: Ibn Hajar (852) in *Fath al-Bari* records that to the *hadith* 'woe to the heels in hell-fire', Abu Dharr added, 'And he did not wipe his feet.'[8]

Al-Qatadah : al-Qurtubi records that al-Qatadah ibn Daamah (117/735) said, 'Allah made required two washings and two wipings.'

iv. ***Arjulikum* : Washing**

Amr ibn Sharhbil al-Shubah : in Ibn Mundhir. He is recorded as saying, 'The Quran came down with wiping but the Sunna is for washing.'

Al-Thalab : Ibn Manzur in *Lisan al-Arab* cites Abu al-Abbas al-Thalab (291/903) as saying, 'The Quran came down revealing wiping but the Sunna is for washing.'[9]

Anas : al-Qurtubi records that Al-Hajjaj ibn Yusuf al-Thaqafi (95/714), governor of the eastern provinces, 'gave a *khutbah* in Ahwaz and mentioned *wudu*. He said, "Wash your faces and hands and wipe your heads and feet because there is nothing of the sons of Adam closer to filth than his feet, so wash them, their bottoms and their tops, and their tendons." Anas ibn Malik heard that and said, "Allah spoke the truth and Hajjaj spoke a lie, because Allah said, Wipe your heads *wa arjulikum*. When he wiped his feet, he (simply) moistened them".' Al-Qurtubi also records, 'It is also reported from Anas that he said the Quran was sent down with wiping but the Sunna is with washing.' Ibn Mundhir records the above from Ibn Umar and also records, '*haddathana* Ismail *haddathana* Abu Bakr *haddathana* Muhammad ibn Abi Adwi from his father that Anas used to wash his hands and feet until they dripped.'

Ibn Kathir records the same story about Hajjaj: 'Ibn Jarir said *haddathani* Yaqub ibn Ibrahim *haddathana* Ibn Uliyah *haddathana* Hamid who said Musa ibn Anas said to Anas, when we were with him, O Abu Hamzah, Hajjaj gave us a *khutbah* in Ahwaz, while we were with him and he mentioned purification. He said, "Wash your faces and wipe your heads and feet because there is nothing of the sons of Adam closer to filth than his feet, so wash them, their bottoms and their tops, and their tendons." Anas heard that and said, Hajjaj spoke a lie: Allah said, *Wipe your heads wa arjulikum*. When Anas wiped the feet, he moistened them. The chain is authentic.' Ibn Kathir also confirms: 'Ibn Jarir said *haddathana* Ali ibn Sahl *haddathana* Mumal *haddathana* Hammad *haddathana* Asim about the case of Anas, and he said. The Quran came down with wiping but the Sunna is for washing. This too has an authentic chain.'

v. ***Arjulukum* : Wash and Wipe**

Hasan (combine): al-Zamakhshari records that Hasan said, 'It is a combining of two matters.' He also records, 'Hasan recited *arjulukum* with *raf*, with the meaning *wa arjulukum*, washed or wiped to the ankles'.[10]

Dawud (combine): al-Razi records that Dawud al-Isfahani al-Zahiri obligates combining the two; it is also the position of al-Nasir of the Zaydis.

Al-Nahhas (combine): al-Qurtubi records, 'al-Nahhas said one of the best things said about the issue is that wiping and the washing are both obligatory together, so the wiping is obligatory because of the recitation of one who recites *nasb*, and the two recitations have the status of two verses.'

vi. ***Arjulikum* or *Arjulakum* : Wash or Wipe**

Al-Tabari (choice): al-Qurtubi records that 'Ibn Jarir al-Tabari (310/922) judged that required for the feet is to choose between the washing and the wiping.' Al-Razi adds that this was Hasan al-Basri's position too, recording, 'The position of Hasan al-Basri and Muhammad ibn Jarir al-Tabari is that the one responsible [for *wudu*] chooses between wiping and washing.'[11]

Ibn al-Arabi al-Maliki records that Muhammad ibn Jarir al-Tabari 'reasoned that the recitation is *arjulikum* with *khafd* in conjunction with the head, so the head and feet are wiped, and the recitation with *nasb* is in conjunction with the face and arms, so they are washed; so in that way it functions in accordance with both recitations.'[12]

Al-Nawawi adds, 'Jubbai, the head of the Mutazilahs, chose between wiping and washing.'[13]

III. Arguments

3.1 Arguments from Sunna

The conclusive argument for the classical Sunni scholars for washing is based on Sunna. A terse argument for washing is that given by Ibn al-Arabi al-Maliki, who says, 'Our proof is the continuous practice [*amal al-mutassil*, that is, from the time of the Prophet (*sallallahu alayhi wa sallam*) to today, of washing the feet] and the multiple unbroken chains of transmitted text [*naql al-mutawatir*]'. Related to this argument for washing is the consensus of the scholars, described by al-Qurtubi as his last proof, namely,

> Consensus [*ijma*]. They agree that the one who washed his feet has in fact fulfilled his obligation, but they disagree about one who has wiped his feet. Certainty is with what they have agreed about and not with what they have disagreed about. The transmitted tradition of all the vast majority [*jamhur*] is from their Prophet (*sallallahu alayhi wa sallam*) that he washed his feet in his *wudu*, once, twice, and thrice, until he had cleaned them.

But while the Sunna is to wash, this was not always the case. Ibn Qudamah reports, 'Said said *haddathana* Hashim that *akhbarana* [it was told us in the form of a report] Ibn Ata from his father that he said *akhbarani* [it was told me in a report] Aws ibn Aws Abi al-Thaqafi that he saw the Prophet come to a *kizamah* [see Notes] of the people of Taif, and he did *wudu* and wiped his feet. Hashim said this was in the initial period of Islam.'[14] Interestingly, the Sunna of washing is so established that when Ibn Manzur cites this *hadith* in order to explain *kizamah* in his dictionary, he says this: 'The *kizamah* is a pipe under the ground and water flows through it. It is mentioned in the *hadith* that the Prophet came to a *kizamah* of the people and did *wudu* with its water and wiped over his *shoes*.'[15]

But besides the argument from Sunna, the classical Sunni scholars also provide numerous arguments for washing based on the Quran. Most of these arguments are linguistic, but some fall into other categories. Let us look at the other categories first.

3.2 Symbolic arguments

Al-Zamakhshari (d.538) in his commentary *Kashshaf* records *wa arjulikum* and says, 'The majority recite *arjulakum* with *nasb*, thereby indicating that the feet are to be washed. If someone asked me why did you [O Zamakhshari] make it recite with *jarr* [that is, *khadf, arjulikum*] and make the admission of a property of wiping [when you actually argue for washing the feet], I would say that the feet are among the three bodily parts washed with a pouring of water on them, so they are places of anticipated wastefulness—that is blameworthy, and actual wastefulness is forbidden—so the feet are placed in conjunction with the third part, which is wiped (i.e., the head), not so as to wipe them, but in order to remind one of the obligation of frugality in pouring water over them.'

So avoiding waste is a consideration which explains away the linguistic inclination toward wiping. This argument relies neither on the Sunna of *wudu* nor on other linguistic possibilities. This is al-Zamakhshari's major argument, and it is repeated by many of the great classical scholars.

Another argument which does not rely on the Sunna nor on linguistic evidence appeals to a sense of symmetry in *taharah*. The argument is recorded by al-Qurtubi in this way:

> Amr al-Shabi said Jibril sent down wiping: Do you not see that *tayammum* has wiping for what was washed [in *wudu*—hands and face] and eliminates what was wiped [in *wudu*—head and feet]?

Ibn Kathir uses this argument too, recording that

> Ibn Jarir said *haddathana* Abu al-Sayb *haddathana* Ibn Idris from Dawud ibn Abu Hind from Shabi that he said, Jibril came down with wiping, then Shabi said, Do you not see that *tayammum* is wiping what was washed and it eliminates what was wiped?

Ibn Qudamah uses this argument as well.

3.3 Linguistic Arguments

Now let us turn to the linguistic arguments. I have collated six different linguistic arguments. These include attempts to show that it is possible in the Arab language (meaning the Arabs have used such a linguistic configuration in the period before and during the descent of the Quran) to have 'your feet' be governed by the initial verb 'wash'.

The first linguistic argument we consider is lexigraphic. Al-Qurtubi records, 'Abu Zayd al-Ansari [215 A. H./830 C. E.] said, wiping in the Arab language is washing and wiping. An example is that the Arab says about someone after *wudu* who has washed the limbs that *tamassaha* [he has wiped].' This argument accepts that 'your feet' is governed by the proximate verb 'wipe', but goes on to posit that 'wipe' in effect means a light washing.

Al-Qurtubi also argues that the word 'wipe' may also apply to 'wash'. However, wipe is usually seen as a subset of wash. The argument of al-Qurtubi is that 'Abd al-Haqq ibn Atiyah (546 A. H./1151 C. E.) said, "There are people among those who recite with a *kasrah* [*khadf*] who judged that the wiping of the two feet is a washing. It is correct that the word wiping shares multiple meanings, applying to wiping and to washing".'

A second argument takes the instances of imperative verb plus a delineated or non-delineated object, as they occur in the verse for *wudu* and for *tayammum*. We have for *wudu* a clear 'wash the hands to the elbows'. When it comes to *tayammum*, we have a clear 'wipe your face and hands'. Based on these instances, the arguments goes, we see that objects governed by the imperative 'wipe' are not given delineations, and the object that is definitely governed by the imperative 'wash' is given delineation, that is, up to something. Therefore, when we come to 'your feet', and we note that they are delineated with 'up to the ankles', we can conclude that the governing verb must be 'wash'. Al-Qurtubi says, 'Allah bounded the area and said *to the ankles* as He said about the arms *to the elbows*. This proves the obligation of washing the feet, but Allah knows best.'

Ibn Hisham in his *Mughni al-Labib* and al-Zamakhshari in his commentary on 5:6 say, 'It was said *to the ankles*, so He mentioned the end-point, and that dismisses the supposition that the feet are wiped, because wiping is not given an end-point in the shariah.'

A third argument is based on the idea that the sequence of bodily parts purified in *wudu*—face, hands, head, feet—is given precedence over syntactical considerations. To illustrate this argument, suppose that the imperatives were given precedence. We would then have, 'Wash your face, hands, and feet, and wipe your head'. But because the head should be washed before the feet, we have, 'Wash face, hands, (but wipe) head, and feet', meaning 'and wash too your feet'.

Al-Qurtubi with this argument, juxtaposes the strong case for wiping based on the Quran and the strong case for washing based on the Sunna. Given this tension he argues that there must be an overriding concern which motivates the inclination of the Quranic phrase towards wiping. That concern, he says, is the sequence.

Al-Qurtubi says,

> And it is said, Allah has *wiped* what you have when He has *washed* and purified you from your sins. So if it is from Arab tradition that the wiping may mean washing, then the statement which preponderates is this statement: if the consequences of the recitation with *khadf* is washing . . . and the many *hadiths* fix washing, and there is the warning not to neglect the washing of the feet in the numerous reports published by the Imams, then the wiping for the head is rather inserted between the things which are washed [arms and feet] for the sake of sequence, that the head should be wiped before the feet are washed, according to this syntax: so wash your faces and your arms to the elbows, and your feet to the ankles, and wipe your heads. But as the

head is done before the feet, it precedes them in the recitation—Allah knows best—not because they share with the head in being wiped, but because the head precedes the feet in the process of purification.

Abu Thawr (d. 240) also explains that there must be some overriding concern which interrupts the list of bodily parts and their imperative verbs. He says that the reason your 'feet is placed' after 'your head' is not because it should take the imperative 'wipe', but because the verse is rather establishing the sequence of *wudu*. He says, 'The munificent verse mentioned something wiped [the head] among the things washed. The custom of the Arab when he mentioned like things and unlike things [e.g., wiped and washed bodily parts] is to gather the like things and then to put the other thing in conjunction to them [last], and that custom is not opposed except for a bounty, and the bounty, here, is the [teaching of the] sequence [of *wudu*].'[16] Ramli [d. 1004] uses this argument too in his commentary to the *Minhaj* called *Nahayat al-Muhtaj*.

A fourth argument is that in the Arab language before the descent of the Quran, there is a kind of poetic sentence which puts two objects into conjunction, but where the second object is not governed by the same verb as the first object. This would explain how the Quranic phrase puts 'your heads' into conjunction with 'your feet', while the first object is governed by 'wipe' and the second is governed by something else, in this case 'wash'

Ibn Manzur argues this way in *Lisan al-Arab*. He says, 'So one who recites it *arjulakum* does so for two reasons. First, in this there are things anterior and things posterior, as if He said, 'Then wash your faces and arms to the elbows, and your feet to the ankles, and wipe your heads', thereby putting things first and putting things last so that *wudu* would be a succession of things one after another. Then, it is as if He meant, 'Wash your feet to the ankles' because His statement *to the ankles* has already proven that is just as we described it [that is, the argument of delineation], so 'your feet' is arranged with washing, as the poet said:

If only your husband had come tomorrow!
Armed with sword, and lance

meaning 'armed with sword, and carrying a lance', where the verb 'carrying' is supplied, as 'armed' is an inappropriate verb for 'lance'.

Ibn al-Arabi al-Maliki uses the same verse to show that the noun of 'feet' may be in conjunction with the word 'head' but not in conjunction with its meaning (that is, 'wipe'), like the poet's verse:

I saw your husband, clamoring
Armed with sword, and lance.

Al-Qurtubi multiplies the examples of this use of language. He says, 'The Arab puts something in conjunction with something with an act which applies to only one of them. The Arab says, "I ate bread, and milk", meaning, "I ate bread and I drank milk".' Another example is the statement of the poet:

I fed them straw, and cold water.

Another example is [from Labid ibn Rabiah]:

The two used the leaves of the cabbage plant, Giving birth
On the banks to her gazelle, and her brood.

Another example is:

I drank milk, and dates and cheese.

'The *taqdir* [the meaning of sentences with ambiguous syntactical elements] is as follows: I fed them straw, and gave them water to drink; the one giving birth on the banks to her gazelle; and the other brooding her ostrich (the ostrich does not 'give birth to' but rather 'broods' the egg); and finally, I drank the milk, and I ate the dates. So, His phrase *Wipe your heads, and your feet* could be in conjunction with washing in spite of the conjunction with wiping, carrying the meaning and purport of washing. But Allah knows best.'

Al-Jurjani (d. 816), al-Zamakhshari's commentator, also uses the poet's verses:

Armed with sword, and lance
And feeding the animal straw, and cold water.

A fifth argument is based on the different instances of *jarr*, which means the vowel 'i' (*khafd*) given to a word because of proximity. Al-Qurtubi finds this in the Quran, where we have, *Sent down to you will be a flame of fire, and smoke* (55:35), where 'and smoke' is *muhasin* (in some recitations), which is *khafd* because of *jarr*, because 'the smoke' means 'fumes', so the meaning is 'sent down to you will be *smoke*, and a *flame* of fire', where *smoke* and *flame* are the direct objects of the sentence, even though *smoke* is in *khafd*.

Also, al-Qurtubi adds, 'He said, *No, it is a glorious Quran, in a tablet preserved*' (85:21-2). Here *preserved* is *mahfuz-in*, which is *khafd* because of *jarr*. In this sentence, *quran-un, majid-un*, and preserved are all nominatives (*raf*), so that one would say, 'It is a Quran, it is glorious, and it is preserved, in a tablet', but instead of *mahfuz-un*, we have *mahfuz-in*, which is explained as being from proximity to *fi lawh-in* (in a tablet).'

Al-Qurtubi also cites Imru al-Qays, who said:

kabir-u unas-in fi bijad-in muzammal-i[17]

meaning, 'He is great among the people, in his striped garment, wrapped up.' Al-Qurtubi remarks, '*muzammal-i* is made *khafd* by proximity, because "wrapped up" refers to the man, not to the striped garment, so that its inflected termination would otherwise be *raf*".'

He also says, 'It is like the Arabs say, *hadha juhr-u dabb-in kharib-in* [this hole of a lizard, deserted]. The word *kharib-in* [deserted] is made *jarr* even though it would be *raf*.' That is, the sentence reads, 'this deserted hole of a lizard.' He says, 'This is the position of Akhfash and Abu Abidah, but al-Nahhas rejected it and said this statement is a great error, because it cannot be that the proximate be brought into relationship with something in such a sentence, but it is really an error, like changing the vowel to achieve a rhyme.'

Ibn Kathir remarks that the recitation with *khafd* is 'produced because of proximity and the relationship [to wipe your heads] in the sentence, as in the Arab's sentence *juhr-u dabb-in kharib-in*, and as in His statement, *They will have on them clothes of silk, green, and brocade* [76:21]. This is common in the language of the Arab.'

The grammarian Ibn Hisham says, 'A word gives governance to another word when it is in proximity to it, like the statement of some of them: *hadha juhr-u dabb-in kharib-in* with *jarr* but most of them make it *raf*.' That is, *kharib-un*; this is a hole (*juhr-u*), deserted (*kharib-un*), of a lizard (*dabb-in*). He also cites Imru al-Qays's verse:

ka-anna abanan fi afanini wadqihi
kabir-u unas-in fi bijad-in muzammali.

Ibn Hisham al-Ansari also argues from a passage in 56:11-22, which reads in part, 'These will be nearest to Allah, in gardens of bliss . . . . Circling them will be ever fresh youth, with goblets, glasses, and cups . . . and fruits . . . and flesh of fowl . . . and black/white eye'.[18] One question in this passage is what governs the phrases. Ibn Hisham notes that some take 'black/white eye' as *jarr*, that is, *hur-in*, so that 'black/white eye' is governed by 'ever fresh youth'. The meaning is then 'ever fresh youth . . . with black/white eye'. But the conjunction could go all the way back to 'gardens of bliss'. Then, we would have 'gardens of bliss', with 'many fruits', and 'flesh of fowl', and *hur-in ayn-in*, which is then read as a synecdoche, as in 'companions with *hur-in ayn-in*'. 'Cups' would be in conjunction with 'ever fresh youth', so that it would be 'ever fresh youth, circling them with cups'. But Ibn Hisham ends his discussion with the comment, 'Actually, the *khafd* of proximity is rare.'

Ibn Qudamah quotes Imru al-Qays's verse which we saw and also:

fa-zalla tuhatu al-lahm min bayni mundij-in
safifa shiwa-in aw qidir-in mu ajjal-i

The meat cooks erred between a well-cooked
grilled row and quick boil

where *qidir-an* (cooked in a pot) is made *jarr—qidir-in—*by being in conjunction with what is proximate, but referring back to *al-lahm* (the meat).

Ibn Qudamah also cites the Quran, where we have *inni akhafu alaykum adhaba yawm-in alim-in* (I fear for you the punishment of a grievous day) (11:26), saying that *alim-in* is *jarr* because of the proximity of 'day', while it is a description of the punishment, which is *nasb* (the direct object), because of its proximity to the proximate *yawm-in*.

But Ibn Manzur questions the occurrence of the *khafd* of proximity as proving 'washing' in this verse by citing Abu Ishaq, the grammarian, who said, 'Making a noun *khafd* because of proximity is not permitted in the Book of Allah, while it is permissible for poetical imagery.'

Al-Razi too, is doubtful about this argument. He says that the *jarr* of proximity means that the 'feet' are the conjunction with 'wipe your heads', and are governed by 'wipe'. He cites the arguments that this *jarr* is not conclusive, saying 'If it is said no, it is not possible to say that this vowel "i" is there just because of proximity [while "feet" is still in conjunction with "wash your faces"], as it is in the statement:

juhr-u dabb-in kharib-in

and the poet's verse:

kabir anas fi bijad-in mazmal-i

we say that is false.' Al-Razi says the above examples may be explained by poetical exigency.

Second, in the above examples, there is no question of ambiguity. In the statement *juhr-u dabb-in kharib-in* the word, 'deserted' cannot be describing the lizard but must be describing the hole. So, he concludes, 'in this verse certainty in the face of ambiguity is not produced.' For al-Razi, the linguistic argument of *jarr* is ultimately inconclusive.

Al-Shawkani cites the possibilities of an argument of *jarr*, but then acknowledges its weakness and sustains an argument from Sunna.[19] He says,

> The ones who argue that washing the feet is not obligatory, argue from a recitation of *jarr* in His statement *arjulikum* being in conjunction with His statement *your heads*. They say *arjulikum* is one of the [three of the] seven recitations[20] which are authentic. There is an argument for the conjunction being with washing the faces, even though it is recited with the *jarr* of the proximate; this has been related by the majority of the Arab[21] Imams, like Sibawayh and Akhfash, but it certainly is very rare; it differs from the obvious meaning and it cannot sustain the contested position. We argue instead that obligatory is carrying the argument with his (*sallallahu alayhi wa sallam*) consistent practice of washing the feet.

Finally, there is an argument that there is an ambiguity in washing or wiping the feet precisely so that the verse can bear two contexts: wash the feet in one context, and wipe the feet when they are shod.

Al-Qurtubi says, 'It has been said that if the *khafd* of the feet rather mentions restrictively wiping them, it could be for when the feet have shoes on. We learn this restriction from the messenger of Allah, as it is not correct about him that he wiped his feet, except when they were shod. So thereby the messenger of Allah explained with his action the context for washing the feet and the context for wiping them. This is a fine argument.'

Ibn al-Arabi al-Maliki also gives this argument, saying 'Or, the meaning of "wiping" could be for the context of wearing shoes, so the two recitations could be for both contexts [bare feet and shod feet], once *nasb* for the bared feet and once *khafd* for the covered feet.'

IV. Ibn al-Arabi's Position

Ibn al-Arabi alludes to this argument when he discusses the *fiqh* disagreement about what to do when wiping over the shoe when there is a tear in the shoe. He says, 'We argue for wiping what emerges, because we were commanded in the Book of Allah to wipe the feet, so when something of the foot emerges, we wipe it.'[22] Thus, there should be no obstacle in wiping the torn shoe where some of the foot sticks out, because the verse's imperative of 'wipe' fits both cases of shod/bare foot.

Ibn al-Arabi reviews the various positions of the ulema, saying, 'The ulema concurred that the feet belong to the bodily parts of *wudu*, but they disagreed about a format of their *taharah*, whether that is through washing, wiping, or choosing between the two.' As we saw, the position of washing is the position of the majority of the classical Sunni scholars; the position of wiping is the position of many companions and successors, including Ibn Abbas, Anas, and Ikrimah; the position of choosing between the two is that of al-Tabari, Hasan al-Basri, Jubbai, Nasir, and Dawud. It is appropriate here to emphasize that Ibn al-Arabi is neither part of the Zahiri school of jurisprudence associated with Dawud and Ibn Hazm, nor is he a part of the Shi'ite school.[23]

Ibn al-Arabi says, 'Our position is choice' and goes on to say 'the combination is best'. This last phrase probably refers to al-Nahhas own position which is characterized by al-Nahhas as 'one of the best things said about the issue'. We saw above that al-Qurtubi recorded, 'al-Nahhas said one of the best things said about the issue is that the wiping and the washing are both obligatory together, so the wiping is obligatory because of the recitation of one who recites with *khafd* and the washing is obligatory because of the recitation of one who recites with *nasb*, and the two recitations have the status of two verses.'

There is an argument of Ibn Hisham found in his classical grammar *Mughni* which holds that the *wa* (and) could have the meaning of *aw* (or). In this case there is a linguistic argument for choice. The argument goes as follows.

> The meaning of the *wa* here could be 'choice'. One of (the poets) said,
>
> They said, Go far away, choosing for her
> patience '*wa*' crying
> She said, Crying is healthier if I want revenge.
>
> The meaning then is patience *or* crying if patience is not joined to crying (that is, patience *and* crying).[24]

Ibn al-Arabi's position embraces two themes, ease and relief of difficulty, based on the verse *We did not make for you in the religion any constriction* (22:78), a verse which begins with *jahidu fi Allahi* (exert for Allah) and suggests the *ijtihad* of effortful exertion to understand the determined properties (*ahkam*) and the many consequences of a polysemantic text.

Wiping and washing are related as two forms of purification, the one being subsumed in the other. Ibn al-Arabi says, 'Know that washing contains wiping from one perspective, so the one who washed has already subsumed wiping in it, just as starlight is subsumed in the sun's light.' He acknowledges too that it is possible to see wiping simply as a synonym for washing, as we saw above, saying, 'The one who has wiped did not wash, except in a position of the one who believes, and quotes the Arabs, that "wiping" is a word for "washing", so they are synonymous.'[25]

In Ibn al-Arabi's *fiqh*, each command which is operative in the outwardness is also operative in the inwardness. The command of this verse, therefore, has an inward dimension. He says,

> The correct meaning of the *hukm* for the inwardness is that wiping is used for whatever specific practices are necessitated and washing for whatever general practices are necessitated.
>
> Because of this, we propounded choice commensurate with the moment, because perhaps you run to a philanthropist for a designated need, on behalf of an individual himself, then that is in a way station of wiping. And perhaps you run to the king for a need diffused over the entire population, or needs, so that that individual would be included in this general public, so this is in a way station of washing in which is subsumed wiping.[26]

Now Ibn al-Arabi investigates the linguistic evidence of the verse. he notes, 'As for the reciting of His statement [*Wash your faces, and your hands to the elbows, wipe your head*] *wa arjulkum* [your feet] [5:6], with either *arjula*, or *arjuli*—on account of the letter *wa*—according to whether the *wa* is in conjunction with "wipe", through *khafd*, or in conjunction with "wash", with the vocalization *arjula*. Our position is that even the recitation *arjula* does not actually contraindicate wiping, because this *wa* may be the 'and of simultaneity', and the 'and of simultaneity' makes the word *arjula*.'

Even though the recitation of *arjulakum* which we noted above, was generally associated with the argument for taking the initial verb 'wash' as the operative imperative, the argument for wiping is still linguistically strong. Ibn al-Arabi then gives examples of the 'and of simultaneity'. He says:

> You say, *qama Zayd wa Umar-an*;[27] and *wa stiwa-al-mau was l-khashabat-an*;[28] and *wa ma anta wa qasat-an min tharid*;[29] and *wa marrartu bi-Zayd wa Umar-an*. You mean, (I passed Zayd) with Umar. And likewise for the one who recites [with *nasb*] *Wipe your heads and your arjula*, with *a*.

So,

> The argumentation of the one who argues for wiping, in this verse, is stronger, because his argumentation shares with the proponent for washing in giving expression to the recitation *arjula*. But one who argues for washing does not share with the proponent for wiping in giving expression to the recitation *arjuli*.

From the verse 'wiping' is stronger, and the proponent for 'wiping' can point to either vocalization for proof.

Among 'our colleagues', Ibn al-Arabi says, there are those who 'preponderate the specific over the general, and among them there are those who would preponderate the general over the specific: all of that absolutely.' Using the metaphor developed above, some of our colleagues always go to a specific philanthropist, and others always go to the king. They are not sensitive to the context, but instead go fixedly and rigidly to one place.

Ibn al-Arabi then says,

> But our position is other than that. We walk with the Real according to a determined property [*hukm*] of the circumstance, so we generalize where He generalized, and we make specific where He makes specific.
>
> We do not initiate a property, because one who initiated a property has already initiated in his self Lordship, and the one who has initiated in himself Lordship has already diminished his servanthood, to the extent of this issue. And if he has diminished his servanthood, to that extent, he shall diminish the divine self-disclosure of the Real in him. And if he has diminished the divine self-disclosure of the Real in him, he has diminished his knowledge through his Lord. And if he has diminished his knowledge through his Lord, he is ignorant about Him to the context he diminished it, because if there should appear to that one, the one who diminished it, a property in the world [the macrocosm] or in his world [the microcosm], he would not recognize it. Because of this, our position is that we do not initiate a property in one fell swoop.

Ibn al-Arabi is completely familiar with the range of arguments produced by the legal scholars of his time. Their arguments generally seek closure and finality—although without exception, the final theme among all the classical scholars is 'But Allah knows best.' That is, even though they desire closure and finality, the classical scholars leave the door open to continuing divine guidance.[30]

The desire to achieve a single and monolithic understanding of Islam is a perennial problem. Every *qadi* who ever insisted on having the right to use *ijtihad* to settle cases, using any of the schools of jurisprudence which best applied for that particular case, was also fighting against the desire of the sultan and state to codify and impose a Procrustean vision of Islam.

So the sum consequence of the polysemantic text of washing/wiping the feet is 'that or perhaps that', or 'this and that'. The more one knows about this verse, the more one is aware of not knowing. For Ibn al-Arabi, the response to 'not knowing'. is not *qiyas* or *ray* but *taqwa*, becoming protected by Allah through doing acts which will protect oneself from His punishment (which is its Arabic definition).

Interestingly enough, the conclusion or last word of Ibn al-Arabi for every issue, then, is *taqwa*, and this is a conclusion which is valid for every level of knowledge. Ibn al-Arabi's treatment of this particular issue is to multiply its polysemantic nature, to increase the possibilities, to deconstruct false closures and *taqayyid*, and the smugness of 'knowing' He seeks to convince his audience that for this and every issue we must void ourselves of Lordship and exaltedness, becoming instead humbly receptive and alert to divine command.

In the mater of purity (*taharah*) in the same verse we have been considering (5:6), Allah says that He does not wish for us any constriction *ma yuridu Allahu li-ajala alaykum min haraj*, but instead, *He wishes to make you pure.* Then, following this verse He tells us to remember our covenant with Him, when we said, 'We hear and obey'. One might gloss here we listen, we hear, and we obey. For Ibn al-Arabi, assumption of lordship on our part, whether openly or not, precludes our listening, hearing, and ultimately, obeying. And right after that, Allah says, *And have taqwa [fear] before Allah; Allah is aware of the bottom of the hearts*! (5:8).

Notes

1. For instance, in *Sunan* Ibn Majah, *kitab al-taharah, ghusl al-araqib*, where we have, *haddathana* (it was told to us in the form of a *hadith*) Muhammad ibn al-Sabbah *haddathana* Abd-Allah ibn Raja al-Makkayy from Ibn Ajlan: and *haddathana* Abu Bakr ibn Abi Shaybah *haddathana* Yahya ibn Said and Abu Khalid al-Ahmar, from Muhammad ibn Ajlan from Said ibn Abi Said from Abi Salamah, who said, Aishah saw Abd al-Rahman while he was doing *wudu* and said, 'Complete liberally [s.b.gh. IV] the *wudu*, because I saw the messenger of Allāh (*sallallahu alayhi wa sallam*) saying, "Woe to the heels in hell-fire".'
2. Foot is *rijl* and feet are *arjul*. The suffix *kum* is the second person plural pronoun 'your'. The vowel in between is determined by grammatical considerations, explained below.
3. Recorded in *al-nashru fi al-qiraat al-ashr*.
4. Citations of Ibn Mundhir are from his *Al-Awsat* (Dar Ṭaybah, 1985), Volume I.
5. All citations of al-Qurtubi are from his commentary on 5:6 in *Al-jami al-ahkam al-Quran*.
6. Citations from Ibn Kathir are from his commentary on 5:6.
7. *Sunan* Ibn Majah, *kitab al-taharah, ma ja fi ghusl al-qadamayn*.
8. Citations from Ahmad ibn Ali Ibn Hajar al-Asqalani are from his commentary on Sahih al-Bukhari, *kitab al-wudu*, from *isbagh al-wudu*.
9. Recorded in the entry on '*m.s.h.*'
10. Citations of al-Zamakhshari are from his commentary on 5:6.
11. Citations from al-Razi are from his commentary on 5:6.
12. Citations of Ibn al-Arabi al-Maliki are from his commentary on Sahih al-Tirmidhi, *abwab al-taharah*.
13. Citations of al-Nawawi are from his commentary on Sahih Muslim, chapter *wujub ghusl al-rijlayn*.
14. Citations of Ibn Qudamah are from *al-Mughni, ghusl al-rijlayn ila al-kabayn*.
15. Ibn Manzur quotes *hadith* for their linguistic content, but he often quotes inaccurately—this is not to criticize Ibn Manzur and his immensely valuable and unique work, but rather to caution the searcher to refer to the works of the *muhaddithun*, those scholars

who painstakingly transmit *hadith*.

16. From a handbook, *Fiqh al-Imam Abu Thawr* by Sadi Husayn Ali Jabr (Dar al-Furqan, Beirut).
17. The editor of the poems of Imru' al-Qays has:

    ka-anna abanan fi afanini wadqihi
    kabiru unasin fi bijadin muzammal.

    Ibn Manzur quotes this verse and says, *aban* is a name of a man, but mentions mountain too; *afafin* from *fann* meaning types or sorts; *wadq* meaning rain clouds; *bijad* meaning a striped garment; and *muzammal* meaning wrapped up. The imagery is the fecund clouds covering the old mountain. The verse could perhaps be rendered:

    Like Aban and its various clouds
    He is great among the people in his striped garment, wrapped up.

    Ibn Hisham says that '*muzammal*' is a description of the great man, so it should really be nominative (*raf*), but it is *khafd* because of proximity. The poem is edited by Muhammad Abul Fadi Ibrahim, (ed.) 1958. *Diwan Imru l-Qays* (Egypt: Dar al-Maarifah). Citations of Ibn Hisham are from *Mughni al-Labib*.
18. The meaning here is that the black pupil is in a black circle (which is blue or brown in blue-eyed or brown-eyed people) inside the white surrounding. Instead of the white, brown, black seen in a brown-eyed person, one sees black/white.
19. Citations of al-Shawkani are from his *Nayl al-awtar*.
20. There are said to be seven variant readings of the Quran in general; in our specific case, there are three.
21. The transliteration 'Arab' here is important, because this does not refer to ethnicity. It is the specific denotation of a scholar of the Arab language, which is the sum of words understood by the tribes of Arabs before and during—but not after—the descent of the Quran, because the revelation is to an Arab audience and is a *hukman arabiyyan* (13:37)—an Arabic determination. This is the specific usage of Ibn Manzur in his *Lisan al-Arab*. Many of the Arab scholars were and are, ethnically non-Arab.
22. *Futuhat al-Makkiyyah*, volume 5 of the critical edition of Uthman Yahya.
23. A comprehensive refutation of claims that Ibn al-Arabi belonged either to the Zahiri school or to Shi'ism is given by Mahmood al-Ghorab in his various works, most recently in 'Muhiddin Ibn al-Arabi Amidst Religions and Schools of Thought' in *Muhyiddin Ibn Arabi:*

A Commemorative Volume, edited by S. Hirtenstein and M. Tiernan (Great Britain: Element Books).

24. Ibn Hisham's *Mughni* (Dar al-Ihya, Indonesia).
25. As we saw, al-Qurtubi records, Abu Zayd al-Ansari said, 'Wiping in the Arab language is a washing and a wiping. An example is that the Arab says about someone after *wudu* who has washed the limbs that *tamassaha* [he has wiped].'
26. Uthman Yahya's critical edition of the *Futuhat* 5:119-20.
27. Zayd stood, and (with) Umar. This phrase is discussed in *Sharh al-Kafiyah*, based on the book of al-Jurjani.
28. In the *Sharh* mentioned in the previous note, Muhammad ibn Hasan al-Radi says, '*Istiwa al-mau wa l-khashabat-an* means the reaching of the water to the wood; the wood [*khashabat*] does not rise over the water; the wood here is the measure by which one knows the degree of rising of the water at the time it is increasing.' The gloss then is, 'The water reached the level with the wood.'
29. 'What do you have to do with the bowl of stew?' This phrase is discussed in the *Sharh* mentioned above.
30. The contrast with modern 'Islamicist' scholarship was apparent here in Islamabad during the (perennial) controversy over moon sighting or calculation last February 1995. In *The News*, a scholar seemingly trained in the classical *fiqh* listed all of the major arguments from the various schools of jurisprudence, but then, instead of ending with *But Allah knows best*, he proceeded to give one narrowly conceived argument as the final word. (It happened to be the 'scientific' answer). Most Islamicist scholarship seems intent on covering up *ikhtilaf* rather than appreciating its presence as a mercy for the *ummah*.

CHAPTER 6

Three Passages from Ibn al-Arabi's Fiqh

There is a great thirst for the direct word of Allah. Knowledge in the Quran is linked with water; rain comes down from the heavens, the parched earth drinks it, and vegetation is produced. Muhammad received the rain, which comes 'freshly from its Lord'. Rain is the direct knowledge which Allah gives to make us whole. River water is indirect knowledge—knowledge from our intellects—which gets mixed up with impurities and is subject to pollution. I used to joke that now we have acid rain: but, now I think that is our situation indeed. We no longer have the direct, clean, pure rainwater which Allah provides because the medium above us is itself polluted.

I have tried here to clear the air of the irritants and obstacles which come in the way of hearing the word directly. What Ibn al-Arabi does, above all, is to prepare his audience for the encounter and then to become transparent before the encounter. His intellect, his genius, and his skill pale in comparison with this gift: a way to hear in clear and clarifying language, the divine word.

And as therefore neither conclusions nor resolutions are appropriate, we take up three passages from Ibn al-Arabi's *fiqh*.

I. The First Passage

In the first passage, we hear Ibn al-Arabi's discussion on *awrah*. This word is not translatable, but it is describable. Classically, *awrah* meant the part of the body, men's and women's, which had to be covered. The classical *fiqh* books spent most of their time discussing the man's *awrah* and the man's clothing. Today of course, *awrah* means the shameful part of women, including their voices, smell, and very presence. In fact, in

Urdu, woman herself is called shameful—*aurat*. In order to recover the direct knowledge of the Quran, let us take up Ibn al-Arabi's discussion here; I have first translated Ibn Manzur's descriptions of key words needed for this passage from Ibn al-Arabi's *Futuhat al-Makkiyyah*.

Awrah (`w.r.): Ibn Manzur says, 'The *awrah* of the man and the woman is their private parts.' And 'the *awrah* is everything that causes embarrassment if it is exposed.' Also, 'The *awar* [`w.r.] has only one eye'. He also says, 'Covering the *awrah* during the *salah* and other than the *salah* is obligatory; about covering it when secluded there is a disagreement'. And 'in the Quran we have, *Our houses are awrah* (33:13), that is, they are open to the thief because the houses have been cleared of the men, but Allah caught them in their lie, saying, *But they were not awrah, they only wanted to desert* [33:13]. It is said its meaning is, Our houses are *awrah*, that is, our houses are near the enemy and we were stolen from them. But Allah knew that their intent was deserting the battle.'

Ibn al-Arabi says, 'The ulema agree that covering the *awrah* is obligatory, with no disagreement, and absolutely, that is, during the *salah* I shall mention its boundary of the man and the woman.'

Mayl (m.y.l.): Ibn Manzur says, '*Mayl* is inclining toward something.'

Ibn al-Arabi says, 'The crossover for that in the inwardness. It is obligatory on every intelligent person to cover the divine secret which, if it were disclosed, would lead someone, who was neither knowledgeable nor intelligent, to a lack of a sense of taboo toward the Side of the divine, Exalted, Forbidden, because the reality of *awrah* is *mayl*. Because of this that person said *Our houses are awrah* [33:13], that is, inclined, bent on destruction, when they sought to desert; then Allah caught them in their lie, before His Prophet, with His word, *But they were not awrah; they only meant to desert* [33:13], that is, to desert what you [Muhammad] called them to. There is also the *awar* [one-eyed man], because his view inclines [m.y.l.] to a single perspective.

'Like that it is appropriate that the knowledgeable one cover from the ignorant one the secrets of the Real; secrets like His word, *There are no whisperings of three except He is the fourth* [58:7]; His word, *We are closer to one than the jugular vein* [50:16]; and His word, *I become his ear, and his eye, and his tongue*, because when the ignorant one hears that, it leads him to forbidden conceptualizations like divine incarnation or bounded divinity. Therefore it is appropriate that with which the Real turns and inclines to the hearts of the knowledgeable ones—Exalted is He and Holy—with His address, be covered up with whatever His Majesty necessitates of Independence absolutely from the worlds; in addition to His word on the tongue of His messenger, *I was hungry and you fed me not, I was sick and you visited me not, I was thirsty and you did not give me to drink.*

'So he covers up the knowledge of this secret from the ignorant one and he does not add to what He said as a commentary to it [that is, *I was hungry*] at all. He covers up as the Real does with His word, *So and so was sick, and if you had visited him, you would have found Me with him.* This is more ambiguous than the first statement, but He gives in this commentary to the ones who know Allah, another knowledge about Him which they did not have. That is that in the first He made Himself the very same sick and hungry one but in His commentary He made Himself the Helper of the sick one, as He is *with him*, because whoever helps the sick one is with him. How far away is this from the One who made Himself the sick one himself! Each statement in that way is real, and to every real [*Haqq*] is a Reality [*Haqqiqah*].'

Ammi (`m.m.): (This is one of the most loaded classical words, usually full of the absolute class distinctions of the elite and the mass. Ibn al-Arabi's use of the word is, however, quite different and is tied into one of the descriptions used by Ibn Manzur). Ibn Manzur says, 'A *ummayy* [`m.m.] man and a *qusriyy* [q.s.r., utmost] man. The *ummay* is the *amm* and the *qusriyy* is the *khass*. In the *hadith*: When he used to go home, he gave upon entrance three *juz*[1]: a *juz* to Allah, a *juz* for his family, and a *juz* for himself. Then he apportioned *juz* for him and the people and he correlated that portion to the *ammah* through the *khassah*, meaning that the *ammah* were not with him at that moment, so the *khassah* communicated to the *ammah* what they heard from him; it is as if the benefits were transferred to the *ammah* from the *khassah*.'

According to Ibn al-Arabi, 'As for the covering up of that before the *ammi*, it is that one say to him about His statement, *You would have found Me with him* that the condition of the sick one is certainly that of dependency and need of the one in whose hand is the cure—and that is no one but Allah, so mostly what we need is to remember [*dhikr*] Allah with each instant to repel what befell him, which is different from the healthy one: He said, *I Myself am seated with the one who remembers* [*dhikr*] *Me*. This is the healthy condition. The *ammi* is satisfied with it and the knowledgeable one stays with what He taught him about that upon his knowledge; this is the cover up of the divine *mayl* from the gaze of the *ammi*.

'The ulema then disagree about whether covering the *awrah* during the *salah* is a precondition for the validity of the *salah* or not. There is one who says that covering the *awrah* is one of the Sunnas [voluntary but customary practices] of the *salah*, and there is one who says that it is one of the obligations of the *salah*.

'As for the crossover for that spiritually, we have already taught you the concept of *awrah* above. About this issue, as it is established [by an authentic *hadith*] that the one praying is in intimate conversation with his Lord and that the *salah* has been divided in two between Allah and His worshipper, so the one who sees predominate [in this issue] that the Real is the One praying through the acts of His worshipper, that is, the outward practices of the worshipper in the *salah*, as it is established that *Verily Allah said on the tongue of His worshipper during the salah, Allah hears the one who praises Him* [*sami Allahu li-man hamidah*], when one rises after *ruku*, and the worshipper is the speaker, certainly; and He said, *Give him [asylum] so that he may hear the Word of Allah* [9:6], while it is the messenger (*sallallahu alayhi wa sallam*) of Allah, who is reciting, certainly; [that one who takes this position says] the covering of the *awrah* is one of the obligations of the *salah*, that is, the likes of this should not be made manifest before the *ammi*, meaning its supra-sensory meaning and its secret, which is known by the knowledgeable one; rather, the *ammi* should believe in it [without understanding it], as is mentioned, *Only the knowledgeable ones will understand it* [29:43].

'And the one who sees that there is no gradation in this issue between the knowledgeable one and the *ammi*, and that there is nothing but what the text relates, and if it causes to lead, before the hearer, towards what it leads to—if he does not go outside of what the language requires for that—even though their degrees are granted preference [one over another], then the covering of the *awrah* in his view is one of the Sunnas of the *salah*, not one of its obligations. *Allah says what is real, and He is the guide of the way* [33:4].

'About the boundary of the *awrah*, there is one who says that the *awrah*, for the man, is the two private parts and there is one who says that it is, for the man, from the navel to the knee. It is, according to us, only the private parts.

'The crossover for that spiritually: whatever is blameworthy, hated, and filthy of humankind is the *awrah* according to Reality. The two private parts are a place for what we mentioned. It is at the location of the unlawful; and in addition to the private parts is what encroaches on the private parts, the navel on the upper and the knee on the lower; the encroaching area is at the location of the Doubtful, and it is appropriate that one protect oneself [w.q.y., cf. *taqwa*] [from the Doubtful], because *The herder going around the enclosed precinct may almost get into it* [and so should stay well away from the boundary of the Unlawful].

'About the boundary of the *awrah* for the woman, there is one who says that all of her is *awrah* except the face and palms and there is one who argues for that and adds that her feet are not *awrah*. And there is one who says that all of her is *awrah*. As for our position, there is nothing *awrah* of the woman, in fact, except the private parts, just as He said, [*their sawah* {*two private parts*} *became visible to them], and they [Adam and Eve] started weaving for themselves the leaves of the Garden* [7:22], so He treated Adam and Eve the same in the covering of the private parts; they are the two *awrahs*. Even though the woman is commanded [in the last shariah, of Muhammad] to cover [more], and that is our position, yet this is not because of it being *awrah*. That [covering of the leaves of the private parts] is a legal property set down by shariah mentioning covering; but it is not necessary that anything else be covered as *awrah*.'[2]

II. The Second Passage

To understand this second passage, we need to understand Ibn al-Arabi's Arabic conception of *sawm*. It will become immediately clear why this word can not be translated, either by 'fasting' or by any conventional Arabic phrase.

Ibn al-Arabi begins his large chapter on the *sawm* with its definition. He says, 'You should know—may Allah strengthen you!—that the *sawm* is *imsak* [abstention] and *rifah* [elevation].' As usual, we turn to the description of the word in *Lisan al-Arab* and find the same: Ibn Manzur says, 'The word *sawm* in the language is *imsak* [abstention] from something and *tark* [leaving] it.' This is the first description. For the second, Ibn Manzur says, 'There is *sama* [from the same three letter root s.w.m. from which the word *sawm* is derived] the day when it draws up and rises to the zenith of mid-way. Imru al-Qays (one of the pre-Islamic poets whose Arabic usage is authoritative) said, *idha sama an-nahar wa hajjara* (the day rose up and became mid-way).'

To demonstrate the second description, Ibn al-Arabi says, 'One says, *sama an-nahar* when the day elevates. Imru al-Qays said, *idha sama an-nahar wa hajjra*, that is, became elevated. Because the *sawm* has been elevated above the rest of the worships [the pillars of Islam, such as *salah* and *zakah*] by a degree, it is called *sawm*. He—Exalted beyond—elevated the *sawm* by refusing any similarity with it to the worships, as we shall explain. He takes the *sawm* away from His worshippers even though they are doing it as a worship and attaches it to Himself—*subhana-hu* [He is exalted beyond]—and gives with His hand the reward to the one with the attribute of *sawm* who does it. He links the *sawm* to Himself by refusing any similarity [of it to the other worships].'

Ibn al-Arabi will explain below why the *sawm* is elevated above the other worships using the same evidence which Ibn Manzur uses. Ibn Manzur says, 'There is a *hadith* where the Prophet (*sallallahu alayhi wa sallam*) said, Allah said, *Every act of the offspring of Adam is theirs, except the sawm, because it is for Me*. Abu Ubayd said, Allah has made the *sawm* special with it being His and as being something which He rewards.'

In fact, the conception of elevation (*rifah*) and abstention (*tark*) both point to the particular description of *sawm*. Ibn al-Arabi says, 'The *sawm* is in reality a *tark*, not a practice, and the refusing of similarity is a negative attribute which intensifies the relationship of the *sawm* to Allah. He said about Himself, *Laysa ka mithlihi shayun* [There is nothing like Me] [42:11], so He refused that there should be to Him a *mithl* [similar], because He—*subhana-hu*—has no *mithl*, according to intellectual and shariah proofs. And al-Nasai [one of the authoritative collectors of *hadith*] published from Abu Umamah that he said, "I came to the messenger of Allah and I asked him, Command me with a command which I can take from you. He said, On you is the *sawm*, because it has no *mithl* [there is nothing like it]." Thus he refused that any of the worships which are made shariah for the worshippers be made similar to it.'

In order to pursue this particular conception, Ibn al-Arabi continues with the usual evidence for this worship. He says, 'And Muslim published in his authentic collection from Abu Hurayrah that he said, The messenger of Allah said, *Every act of this offspring of Adam is theirs, except the sawm; I reward it*. And *siyam [sawm]* is a shield; when there is a *sawm* day for one of you, do not be loud and noisy on that day. If someone insults you or fights you, say, I am one with the matter of *sawm* [*saim*], I am a *saim* [one fasting]. And by the one in whose Hand the soul of Muhammad is, the breath of the one with *sawm* is better, according to Allah, on the day of judgement, than the scent of musk. And the one with *sawm* has two joys which he enjoys: when he breaks [fast] with his *iftar* there is a joy and when he meets his Lord there is a joy in his *sawm*.'

The last phrase is awkward and not an expected turn of phrase. This should be a signal to us that something quite particular is happening. Indeed, taking the conception of *sawm* which Ibn al-Arabi has developed gives an explanation why we have this strange turn of phrase. He says, 'Know that as he refused any similarity with the *sawm*, as was established in what preceded with the *hadith* of al-Nasai and the reality that *Laysa ka mithlihi shayun* [there is nothing like h/Him, 42:11], the *saim* meets with his Lord by the attribute of *Laysa ka mithlihi shayun* and sees Him by it, so He is the Seer who is Seen. Because of this, he said, There is a joy in his *sawm*, and he did not say, There is a joy in meeting his Lord, because the joy is not a joy enjoyed by himself but is a joy enjoyed in *it*. And the one about whom the Real is his eyes with which he sees and witnesses, he himself does not see except by His seeing.'

This last phrase is the thematic *hadith qudsi* which is as follows: 'My *abd* draws near to Me by means of nothing dearer to Me than that which I have established as a duty for him. And My *abd* continues drawing nearer to Me through supererogatory acts until I love him; and when I love him, I become his ear with which he hears, his eye with which he sees, his hand with which he grasps, and his foot with which he walks.'

Concluding, he says, 'So the joy of the *saim* is his meeting at the degree of refusal of similarity. His joy in the *iftar* [breaking of the fast] is in the world, in respect to giving due to the physical self which needs nourishment for itself. As the *abd* is described in this *hadith* as having *sawm*, and deserving the name *saim* because of this description, so after the affirmation of his *sawm* the Real negates it and attaches it to Himself, saying, [Every act of the offspring of Adam is theirs] except the *sawm*; it is Mine [or, it is for Me], that is, an attribute of *samadani* [cf. *Allah us-samad*] [112:2], which is being beyond needing nourishment. "It is Mine only; even though I may describe you with *sawm*, I so describe you by some delimiting metaphor of *tanzih* [being beyond an attribute], not by the absolute *tanzih* which is appropriate to My Majesty. So I say, And I reward it." So the Real rewards the *sawm* for the *saim* when he turns to his Lord and he is cast to his Lord by the attribute of "He has no *mithl*"—which is the *sawm*, as the one to Whom "There is nothing like unto" cannot see anything but one whom "There is nothing like unto." Abu Talib al-Makki—he was one of the masters of the folk of tasting—determined the text—*jaza-u-hu man wujida fi rahl-ihi fa-huwa jaza-u-hu* [12:75][3]—for what this verse requires for this circumstance.'

Now we can turn to the passage in question. 'The most surplusing and balanced *sawm* is "fasting" one day for yourself and fasting one day for your Lord and between them a day breaking fast . . . . But when some of them saw that the right-claim of Allah is more right, they did not see treating equally the right of Allah and the right of the worshipper, so they fasted for two days and broke fast for one day. This was the fasting of Mary, because she saw that *men have a degree over women* [2:228], so she said, Perhaps I shall make this second day of fasting one to counter this degree. And that was how it was, because the Prophet *testified that she was complete* [perfect], just as he testified to the completion of the Men.[4] And when she saw that the testimony of two women was balanced with the testimony of one man, she said, "Two days fasting for me is at the level of one day fasting of the Man." Thus she got the station of the Man for that, and she equalled David in surplus in the fast. So because of this, the one who overcomes in himself his *nafs* has overcome in himself his [tendency to] divinization; then it is appropriate that he treat his *nafs* as Mary treated her *nafs* in this context, lest her *nafs* overtake her *aql*; this is a fine allusion for the one who understands it.'

Dahr: Ibn Manzur says, '*dahr* is an extremely long time'. And 'there is the *hadith, Do not revile the dahr because Allah is dahr*.'

Qayyum (q.w.m.): Ibn Manzur says, 'The *Qayyum*, one of Allah's names; Allah is Standing up by Himself absolutely, not by [the help of] anyone.'

Ibn al-Arabi continues, 'When completion became hers, she caught up to the Men, and the most completion was hers in her catching up to her Lord. It was like Jesus son of Mary, her son, because he used to fast *dahr* and not break the fast, and he used to stay up (q.w.m.) at night and not sleep. Outwardly in the world he was with the name *dahr* in the day and with the name *Qayyum*—the one whom *sleep does not seize, nor slumber* (2:225) at night. So divinity was claimed for him, and it was said, *Allah is the Christ, son of Mary* (5:72), and that was not said about any prophet before him, because the most that was said about Uzayr was that he was the *son of Allah* (9:30). It was not said, He is Allah.'

Kufr: Ibn Manzur says the word *kufr* is derived from *satr* (veil, cover).

Kanaf: Ibn Manzur says, In the *hadith* of Ibn Umar, we have about salvation, The believer draws closer to his Lord on the day of judgement until He places over him His *kanaf*. Ibn Mubarak said, He meant, He covers (s.t.r.) him.

'So look at what effect this [divine] attribute had,' Ibn al-Arabi says, 'from behind the veil of the unseen, on the hearts of the veiled ones of the folk of disclosure such that they said, *Allah is the Christ, son of Mary* [5:72]; *kufr* is related to them for that,[5] set up as an excuse for them, because they did not commit *shirk*; rather they said, *He is Allah*, and the one who commits *shirk* is the one who makes with Allah another god. So this is one doing *kufr*, not *shirk*. Therefore He said, *They have done kufr who say, Allah is the Christ, son of Mary*, thereby attributing to them a *sitr* [a cover, that is, *kufr*]; they took the humanity of Jesus to be a locus of divine manifestation [*majalla*]. Jesus warned him[self] about this station, in what Allah reported, as a confirmation for them concerning what they said. Christ said, *O Bani Israil, worship Allah, my Lord and your Lord.* They said, That is what we are doing! So they worshipped Allah through him. Then He said to them, *The one who commits shirk with Allah, Allah has made forbidden to him the Garden* [5:72], that is, Allah has made forbidden His *kanaf* with which He covers [s.t.r.] him; but Allah already described them with being covered [s.t.r.] in that He described them with *kufr*. This is a verse whose literal meaning gives exactly that which the matter itself gives of that. The *tawil* [allegorical interpretation] of the verse is caught up in blameworthiness; if you comprehend what we have mentioned about it, you will fall into the great ocean and you will not be saved from drowning in it at all, because it is the endless ocean. There is no deeper[6] word of Allah for the one who sees it and has eyes to see it and is from Allah concerning it *upon insight* [12:108].'[7]

III. The Third Passage

Ibn al-Arabi says, 'Abu Ahmad mentioned in a *hadith* of Abd-Allah ibn Buayl ibn Waraqa al-Makki from Amr ibn Dinar from Ibn Umar from Umar that he vowed to sit (`k.f.) in the sacred mosque, and the messenger of Allah (*sallallahu alayhi wa sallam*) said to him, Sit in *itikaf* and do *sawm*.'

Awliya: Ibn Manzur says, 'The *waliy* [singular of *awliya*] of the right hand is the one who is in charge of one's command and executes his tasks.'

'Its connecting crossover: Rasululah, the messenger of Allah commanded the one desiring to stand [q.w.m.] with Allah that they should stand with him by the attribute which is Allah's, and that attribute is the *sawm*, so that one should be with Allah, by Allah, for Allah, so nothing of them would be seen except Allah. This is the circumstance of the folk of Allah. It was asked of the Rasululah, Who are the *awliya* of Allah? He said, *Those who, when they are seen, Allah is remembered [dh.k.r.,* cf. *dhikr*], that is, in order to be made real by Allah they disappear in him from them and from the eyes of creation, so when the people see them, they see nothing but Allah, so their remembering of Allah is their seeing the *awliya*. It is like the above-mentioned verses. This is the station which the Rasululah asked for in his prayer, *And make me nur* [n.w.r.], and Allah answered his prayer, as we were told that he was sent to people *as one of good tidings, warning, calling to Allah by His leave, and an illumined lamp* [*siraj munir*, n.w.r.] 33-45-6; so He made him *nur* as he asked.

'His word to his Lord, *And make me nur*, was, So that I would be in my essence the very divine name itself *al-nur*, and the one whom the Real is *his ear, his eye, his tongue, his hand, and his foot*; and one who *would not speak from caprice* [53:3]. So he is not he, and nothing remains for the one who sees him, who sees him, except Allah, that being known by the one who sees or not; this is the way the folk of knowledge of Allah witness him.

'Among the believers there are the *khulafa* [kh.l.f., ones representing someone behind them, singular *khalifah*] who manifest in the world and among the masses with the attributes of the one who is behind [kh.l.f.] them. Bilqis [the queen of Sheba] said about her throne, *ka'anna-hu huwa*,[8] but it was nothing but *huwa* [it/Him]! But her veil was the extreme distance [between her palace and Solomon's] and the force of convention [which says thrones do not transport themselves across large distances instantly], and she was unaware of Solomon's power with his Lord, so this veiled her from saying, *huwa huwa* [it is It; he is He; etc.]. So she said, *ka'anna-hu huwa*. And what distance could be greater than one to whom *there is no mithl* [like] compared to one whose *mithl* is things? The complete one [Muhammad] said, *Indeed I myself am a human being who is your mithl* [like yourselves]—this based on a command of Allah. It was said to him, *Say,* and he said, *Say*: *indeed I myself am a human being who is your mithl* [41:7], and by this we know that it is based on a command of Allah, because he conveyed the command to us just as he conveyed what was commanded.

'This statement is a remedy for the sickness which arose in the one who worshipped Jesus in his commentary; they said, *Indeed Allah is the Christ, son of Mary* [5:72], missing a great knowledge in that they said *son of Mary* and they did not realize. Because of this, Allah said in raising proof against the one with this description [the *mushrik*], *Say: Name them* [that is, name the partners of Allah, 13:33], but they could not name him [e.g., *Allah, the Christ, son of Mary*] except by one of the names they knew him by, in order that he understand from them what they meant, because when they gave them [the partners] names, it became clear, in the name itself [*Allah, the Christ, son of Mary*], that he was not one of the messengers who were sent demanded that they worship.

'But we rather said, *huwa huwa* [h/He is He] based on what sound disclosure gives the *khass* and what clear faith gives the *amm*, just as the prophetic report from the divine relates, that Allah, when He loves His worshipper, He becomes his ear, his eye; and He mentions his faculties and limbs. And humankind is nothing but these faculties and limbs which the Real makes his he-ness itself.[9] So if you are a believer, do you know what you believe in? And even if you are one with a sound vision, do you know what you saw? Most of this prophetic explanation about Allah is concerned with the human faculty so that the believer would be one with a state of seeing, so that one would know by that the One who is the entity itself of the things and the entities.'

Notes

1. Ibn Manzur says, '*juza*' in the 'arabic discourse is the *nasib* (share of profit, portion)'.
2. This passage is found in volume six.
3. This brilliant reading works from the literal meaning of this verse. The context is Joseph's brothers' plot, where they planted the cup in Joseph's saddle bags. The Egyptian guards are saying, 'What should the *jaza* (recompense) be if you all have lied?' They say, *jaza-u-hu man wujida fi rahl-i-hi fa-huwa jaza-u-hu* (12:75). Contextually, they are saying, 'The recompense (punishment) for stealing the cup shall be the one in whose saddle bags the cup is found—he is its recompense (he shall pay for it).' Because of Arabic grammar (and this is prevalent throughout the Quran), the phrase is ambiguous. Who is the 'it' of 'his' referring to? (One mystic approach is to play out the ambiguities; phrases like 'Adam was created upon His/his form' literally admit of two different interpretations). The phrase can be also phrased: H/his reward is the O/one in whose saddle bags H/he is found—H/he is His/his reward. Abu Talib's phrasing here is, The One who is found, He is his reward. That is, for the joy of the *saim*, only the One who has no like can see the One who has no like, so He finds Himself and He is His own reward.
4. I capitalize this 'm' because Ibn al-Arabi is using 'Men' in the general sense. That is, 'Men' can be complete/perfect because of this prophetic statement. For Ibn al-Arabi, the fact that a Woman has been testified to be czomplete is sufficient proof that a woman may lead the *salah* in congregation with men, something absurdly shocking to contemporary Muslims.
5. The verse is, *la-qad kafara alladhina qalu inna Allah huwa al-masihu*

bnu Maryam, 'They have done *kufr* who say, Allah is the Christ, son of Mary.'

6. One short section of Ibn Manzur's description of the semantic field of this multifaceted word includes: 'Allah said, *We gave him hukm as a child*, that is, knowledge and understanding, this said about Yahya ibn Zakariyya [John the Baptist], and likewise the poet's verse, Silence is a *hukm*, with little activity [Still waters run deep], and in a saying, In poetry is a *hukm*, that is, in poetry are words which benefit.' Hence with the proximity of the endless or bottomless ocean, I translated *ahkam* as 'deeper'.
7. This passage is from volume nine.
8. *ka-anna-hu huwa* can be variously rendered, It is as if it is it; It is as if He is He; It is as if he is He, and so on.
9. The phrase is delightfully gendered: *huwiyyat*, he-ness, is feminine!

Afterword

Whenever I have to explain my wide-ranging interests, I end up saying that I am interested in languages. I am interested in how languages work, how we use language, and how we deal with languages which are divine and revealed. This book has been an exploration of language, focusing on the legal-spiritual-discursive language of *fiqh*, and especially that of Ibn al-Arabi.

One can be excused for believing that it is only postmodern art and scholarship which recognize that languages are opaque and that it is not a transparent medium through which Being shines, as Edward Said said. In fact, the mystics and the sufis have been extremely concerned with language and with reflection on language. Michael Sells' book, *The Mystical Languages of Unsaying*, demonstrates the attention mystics have paid to language, to use its limitations to express things that are un-things and to say things that are un-sayable. The non-mystics who heard the mystic, were distressed by the idea that their language and indeed their religion (even their religion, that religion made by themselves), was not ultimate. The moderns who hear the postmoderns also get distressed.

Foucault talks of this distress felt by those who perceive that his project, which he defines as follows,

> To determine, in its diverse dimensions, what the mode of existence of discourses and particularly of scientific discourses (their rules of formation, with their conditions, their dependencies, their transformations) must have been in Europe, since the seventeenth century, in order that the knowledge which is ours today could come to exist, and, more particularly, that knowledge which has taken as its domain this curious object which is man.[1]

challenges their sense that discourse 'can be a seat of insubstantial immortality'.[2] Coming up against the truth that their, and his language is not ultimate but in fact is a prisoner to 'an obscure set of anonymous rules',[3] Foucault says,

> So many things, in their language, have already escaped them; they do not mean to lose, in addition, *what they say*, that little fragment of discourse—speech or writing, it matters little—whose frail and uncertain existence is necessary to prolong their life in time and space. They cannot bear—and one can understand them a little—to be told: discourse is not life; its time is not yours; in it you will not reconcile yourself with death; it is quite possible that you have killed God under the weight of all that you have said; but do not think that you will make, from all that you are saying, a man who will live longer than he. In each sentence that you pronounce—and very precisely in the one that you are busy writing at this moment, you who have been so intent, for so many pages, on answering a question in which you felt yourself personally concerned and who are going to sign this text with your name—in every sentence there reigns the nameless law, the blank indifference: 'What matter who is speaking; someone has said: what matter who is speaking'.[4]

For Ibn al-Arabi, for the Sufis and the mystics and the Sufi scholars, the universe itself is Words of Allah. Evidence profferred includes Jesus, who was *His [Allah's] word [kalimah] bestowed on Mary* [4:171]; and *If all trees on earth were pens and the oceans ink, with seven oceans behind it to add to its supply, yet the words [kalimat] of Allah would not be exhausted* (31:27); and *To Him mount up the words [kalim] of purity, and He raises each practice of righteousness* (35:10). The definitive proof is, *We say to a thing, when We want it to be, We say to it, Be! and it becomes* (16:40). Things get very interesting when these Words hit the world of human beings; the imagery of Jesus as Word of God, of Muhammad as the pure tablet, that is, Mary, receptacle of divine Word (Jesus/Quran).

The discourse that Foucault is talking about, and that the mystics are warning us about, wants to become God, wants to conquer death. It is religion in general, the man-made construction of rules and regulations that will ensure if not happiness in life (that is the job of the religion of science and technology) but at least happiness in the next life. What kept the scholars of Islam—at least many of them (but not so many now)—safe from this language-idol was the concept of *ikhtilaf*, disagreement. That finite number of *fiqh* positions, a few hundred and no more, is the sum of the legal description of Islam: and every one of those few hundred positions are disagreed about. Every act of human beings is immersed in ambiguity and every act therefore has *ikhtilaf* in its prescriptions.

The word *ikhtilaf* is a reflexive form of *khilaf*, to be against, opposite, or facing. The concept means that if you say, 'Covering the head is obligatory on the man during the *salah* (ritual prayer)', someone else, in the mode of *ikhtilaf*, will say, 'Covering the head is not obligatory'. Now add to the legal description a novel situation (*hal*) and the *hukm* changes. Something appropriate in one situation is inappropriate in another. Is lying wrong? Yes, in this situation. No, in that situation. Like Tevke in the *Fiddler on the Roof*, 'on the one hand' and 'on the other hand'.

Any honest reading of the classical *fiqh* should cure once and for all the idea that Islam is monolithic, monocultural, and monomeaning. The phrases 'Islam says' or 'Islam is', would never again appear on one's lips. Language carries with it ambiguities, and the *fiqh*, immersed in language, community, and debate, concerned with wisdom, judgement, and appropriateness, has embraced, and ought to again embrace that ambiguity.

When first confronted with this fundamental ambiguity of *fiqh*, many Muslims will surely get nervous and distressed. They might think that embracing ambiguity will send them over the brink to hedonism or nihilism, because if a particular activity is not the only truth, maybe nothing is true. The concept of multiple truths, however, means that activities can be mutually exclusive, firmly in the ambiguity of *ikhtilaf*, and be meaningful.

Grossly oversimplifying, one might say that pre-modern societies see the universe as fundamentally uncontrollable, capricious, and not at all scary. Modern, scientific societies see the universe as controllable, laid bare, and occupying second place to man-made forces, buildings, and discourses. Postmodern science returns to the universe as a place of unpredictability, randomness, chaos, and magic. Historically and thematically, Islamic civilization dealt with these issues in the form of the Mutazilah and Ashari doctrinal debate, where the Mutazilah position is that the universe is a predictable place because Allah created natural laws that are subject to human discovery; events are subject therefore to human manipulation. The Ashari position in contrast says that every action and every event is a miracle. Things generally do fall when dropped of course, but in every act of gravity is an act of God, and God may occasionally choose to make dropped things rise. It is no coincidence that modern Muslims want to revive Mutazilah positions and that Sufis stick to the orthodox Ashari tenants.

Both positions allow for seeing the divine 'behind' the physical workings of the world. But the Ashari position sets up a framework that sees more clearly and insistently the living God and the living Law. As with fractal geometries, Escher's drawings, and chaos theories, the universe is not less orderly and meaningful just because it does not admit of manipulation and prediction. Let us leave it at that for now: the ambiguous world of *fiqh* is not less meaningful because it refuses reification but more meaningful because it is unrestricted to follow the living divine command. The universe is not predictable except by Allah; but it is meaningful, disclosing patterns and truths. The inarticulate stones know this and 'speak' accordingly: *They praise Him, the seven heavens and the earth and what is in them; there is no thing but it praises Him with His praise, but you do not understand their praise* [17:44].

Notes

1. Michel Foucault, in Graham Burchell (ed.) (1991). *The Foucault Effect* (Chicago: The University Press).
2. Ibid.
3. Ibid.
4. Ibid.

Index of *Hadith* Quotations

And make in my heart a *nur* (light). 95. Bukhari, *Daawat* 9, etc. Wensinck (1969). *Concordance et indices de la Tradition Musulmane*, Volume 7:20.

Are you a Haruri? 17, in Ibn Manzur *Lisan al-Arab*, entry for Harura.

Do not revile the *dahr*, because Allah is *dahr*. 93. Bukhari, *Adab*. Wensinck.

Every act of the children of Adam is theirs but *sawm*, and it is mine. 91. Muslim, *Siyam*, etc. Wensinck.

I am according to the impression of My creature, so let his impression of Me be Good. 59. Bukhari, *Tawhid*, etc. Wensinck.

I was hungry and you fed me not, I was sick and you visited me not, I was thirsty and you did not give me to drink. 88. Muslim 45:43, etc. See William Graham (1977). *Divine Word and Prophetic Word in Early Islam* (The Hague: Mouton).

I have divided the *salah* into halves. 49,89.

Allah says, I have divided the *salah* into two halves, between Me and My creature, and My creature shall have what he asks. When the creature says, *al-hamdu li'-Llah rabb al-alamin*, Allah says, My creature has praised Me . . . . recorded in Muslim, *Musnad*, Tirmidhi, *Muwatta'*, Nasa'i and Abu Dawud. See Graham (1977).

I become his ear with which he hears. 47,87,92,96.

The messenger of Allah said that Allah said, One who takes My *waliy* as an enemy I declare war on him. My creature does not draw near Me with anything more dear to Me than what I made required of him. My creature then continues to draw near Me with supererogatory prayers until I love him, and when I love him, I become the ear with which he hears, and his eye with which he sees, and his hand with which he grasps, and his foot with which he walks. If he asks Me, I give it to him. If he seeks My protection, I protect him. I do not hesitate to do something as I hesitate to take the soul of the believer who hates death, as I hate to harm him. See William A. Graham (1977) *Divine Word and Prophetic Word in Early Islam* (The Hague: Mouton). Also, Sahih Bukhari.

I myself am seated with the one who remembers Me. 88.

My creature rushes to Me on his own; I forbid him the Garden. 58-9. *Sunan al-Nasa'i, al-jana'iz, man qatala nafsahu.*

O people, hear, understand, and know that Allah has worshippers neither prophets nor martyrs whom the prophets and martyrs will be jealous of over their seating places and their proximity to Allah. 62. *Musnad hadith* number 22969, Volume 8 (*Dar al-Fikr* edition 1991), from Abi Malik al-Ash'ari.

The best of you are the ones who, when they are seen, Allah is remembered. 62. Sunan of Ibn Majah, *zuhd, hadith* number 4119, *haddathana* Suwayd ibn Sa'id *haddathana* Yahya ibn Sulaym from Ibn Khuthaym from Shahr ibn Hawshab from Asma' binti Yazid that she heard RasuluLlah *(sallaLlahu alayhi wa sallam)* . . .

The man written down in the scrolls will not enter the fire, even though he is one of the ones of great sins, if there was nothing with him but *la ilaha illa Allah* in all his Islam in his period of life in the world. Cf. Sunan Ibn Majah, *zuhd*, chapter 35, *hadith* number 4300.

The herder going around the enclosed precinct may almost get into it. 89. Bukhari, *Bayu* 2. Wensinck .

The believer is to the believers as the brick wall. 59. Sunan al-Nasai, *zakah, ajr al-khazin.*
There will be a people on the day of judgment the prophets will be jealous of. 52.

Musnad *hadith* number 22969, Volume 8 (*Dar al-Fikr* edition 1991), from Abi Malik al-Ash'ari, that RasuluLlah *(sallaLlahu alayhi wa sallam)* said, O people, hear, understand, and know that Allah has worshippers neither prophets nor martyrs whom the prophets and martyrs will be jealous of.

There shall be no harming . . . Wensinck. 3:499

They will exit who have in their hearts the least, least of a grain of mustard of faith. 60. Graham 124.

Those who, when they are seen, Allah is remembered. 52, 62, 94.

Sunan of Ibn Majah, *zuhd, hadith* number 4119, *Haddathana* Suwayd ibn Sa'id *haddathana* Yahya ibn Sulaym from Ibn Khuthaym from Shahr ibn Hawshab from Asma' binti Yazid that she heard RasuluLlah *(sallaLlahu alayhi wa sallam)* saying . . . The best of you are the ones who, when they are seen, Allah is remembered.

Verily Allah said on the tongue of His creature, Allah hears the one who praises Him. 89.

Bukhari, *Adhan*, etc. Wensinck.

A woman shall not lead a man. 40.

Subul al-Salam.

When the *qadi* judges and does *ijtihad*, and hits the mark, he has ten rewards; and when he does *ijtihad* and errs, he has one or two rewards. 53.

Musnad Ibn Hanbal.

When the people take their places in the Garden, they are called to a vision. 59.

Tirmidi, sifat al-jannah. See James Winston Morris. *Lesser and Greater Resurrection* in Chowdkiewicz, et al. (1988). *Les Illuminations de La Mecque* (Paris: Sindbad).

Who practises a Sunna that is good, and it is practised after him, he gets its reward and the like of the reward of theirs, without diminishing their rewards at all, 61. Sunan Ibn Majah, *muqaddimah*, chapter 14, *hadith* number 207.

Who drinks poison, and kills himself, sips it in the fire of *Jahannam* everlastingly, abiding therein everlastingly. 58.

Who approaches Me an inch. 58.

Musnad Ibn Hanbal, *hadith* number 10228, from Abu Hurayrah, from the prophet, that he said, Allah said, My creature is upon his impression of Me and I am with him when he calls Me; if he calls Me in his self, I call him in My self; if he calls Me in a gathering, I call him in a better and more pleasant gathering. If he approaches Me a handspan, I approach him an armspan, and if he approaches Me an armspan, I approach him an outstretched span. If he comes to Me strolling, I come to him hastening.

Who kills himself. 58-9.

Sunan al-Nasa'i, *al-janaiz, man qatala nafsahu.*

Woe to the heels in hell-fire. 66, 69.

Sunan Ibn Majah, *kitab al-taharah*, chapter 55, *ghusl al-araqib, haddathana* Muhammad ibn al-Sabbah *haddathana* Abd-Allah ibn Raja' al-Makkayy from Ibn Ajlan: and *haddathana* Abu Bakr ibn Abi Shaybah *haddathana* Yahya ibn Sa'id and Abu Khalid al-Ahmar, from Muhammad ibn Ajlan from Sai'id ibn Abi Sa'id from Abi Salamah, who said, Aishah saw Abd al-Rahman while he was doing *wudu* and said, 'Complete liberally [s.b.gh. IV] the *wudu*, because I saw the messenger of Allah *(sallallahu alayhi wa sallam)* saying, 'Woe to the heels in hell-fire'.

Index of Quranic Quotations

Ch./Verse	Page nos.
2:228	93. . . . [To the {women} there is similar benefit to what is against them] and to the men there is against them a degree . . .
2:255	93. . . . Slumber does not seize Him, nor sleep . . .
3:114	58. . . . And they hasten to Good things . . .
4:105	53. We sent down to you the Book in truth, in order that you all would [use it as a *hukm*] between the people, by what Allah shows you . . .
4:148	6. Allah loves not evil broadcast in discourse, except on account of injustice . . .
4:171	100. . . . His Word cast to Mary . . .
5:6	x, 46, 66, 73, 80, 83. O you who believe, when you stand for *salah*, wash your faces, and your hands to the elbows, and wipe your heads, and your feet to the ankles . . . Allah does not want to make against you any constriction, but He wants to purify you and to complete His favour to you, so that

you would be thankful.

5:72 93, 95, 97.
They have done *kufr* who say, Allah is he, the Christ, son of Mary. The Christ said, O children of Israel, worship Allah, my Lord and your Lord. Verily, the one who does *shirk* of Allah, Allah has forbidden him the Garden . . .

7:156 57.
. . . My punishment, I strike it on whom I wish, but My mercy encompasses everything . . .

8:17 21, 31, 33.
You did not kill them but Allah killed them, and you did not throw, when you threw, but Allah threw . . .

9:6 89.
If any of the *mushriks* ask you for asylum, let them, so that he may hear the Word of Allah . . .

9:102 56.
. . . They have mixed a good act with another that was bad.

9:122 vii, 36, 43.
Nor should the believers go out all together; if a group from every expedition stayed, they could get to know the religion and warn their people when they returned . . .

9:30 93.
The Jews call Uzayr a son of Allah . . .

11:123 55.
. . . To Him returns the entirety of the affairs, so worship Him and rely on Him; your Lord is not Unaware of what you are doing.

12:75 92.
They said, The penalty should be that he in whose

saddlebag it is found, should be held to recompense . . .

12:108 94.
Say, This is my way. I invite to Allah upon insight, I and the one who follows me . . .

13:11 21.
. . . Verily, Allah does not change what is with a people until they change what is in themselves . . .

13:33 95.
. . Say, But name them . . .

14:47 60.
Never think that Allah will fail His promise to the messengers . . .

16:40 100.
For the anything which We have willed, We say, Be, and it is.

17:23 43.
Your Lord has determined that you [shall] worship none but Him . . .

17:44 102.
The seven heavens and the earth, and all the beings therein, celebrate Him; there is no thing but it celebrates Him with His praise, but you do not understand their praising . . .

18:66 33.
So they found one of Our *abds* [*abdan min ibadina*] on whom We had bestowed a Mercy from Us, and We taught him knowledge from Our own presence [*ladunna*]

18:79-82 46.
As for the boat . . .

21:105	49. We wrote in the *Zubur* [Psalms], after the *dhikr*, that My right worshippers shall inherit the earth.
22:78	79. . . . He has not made against you in the religion any constriction . . .
24:10	47. If Allah had not given you surplus and His mercy; Allah is Turning [in forgiveness], *Hakim*.
29:43	89. And such are the similitudes We strike for people, but they only understand them who are Knowledgeable.
31:27	100. And if all the trees on earth were pens and the ocean [ink] with seven oceans behind it to add to it, yet would not the Words of Allah be exhausted . . .
33:4	36, 89. . . . But Allah says the truth and is the guide of the way.
33:45-6	95. O prophet, We sent you as a witness, bringer of good tidings, warner, inviter to Allah with His permission, and a lamp, illumined.
35:10	100. . . . To Allah mount up Words of Purity . . .
37:95-96	47. He said, Do you worship what you carved? Allah has made you and what you do/make.
41:7	95. Say, I am a human being like you all . . .

42:11	39, 91-2. . . . There is nothing (like) His like . . .
50:16	87. . . . We are nearer to him than his jugular vein.
53:3	95. Nor does he articulate from his caprice.
55:29	44, 47. . . . Every day He is upon some affair.
57:21	58. Be foremost in seeking forgiveness . . .
58:7	87. . . . There is no secret conversation among three but He is the fourth . . .
59:7	54. . . . So take what the messenger gives you . . .
60:10	47. . . . That is for you the *hukm* of Allah, for determining the *hukm* between you . . .
75:2	49. I swear by the self-reproaching self [*nafs*].
89:27	49. O self [*nafs*] settled.
112:2	92. Allah the Everlasting.

Abd al-Raziq, Ali, 8-9, 14.
Al-Azhar, 48.

Index

Al-Bayhaqi, 41.
Al-Hajjaj, 56, 69.
Al-quddus, 55.
Amish, 39.
Amm, 88, 96.
Aql, 49, 93.
Arkoun, Mohammad, 7, 13.
Asharis, 62, 101.
Asl / usul, 55, 58.
Awliya, 51-2, 62-3, 94.
Awrah, 62, 86-7, 89-90.
Ayubi, 8, 12, 14.

Batin, 17, 20, 31-2.
Batiniyyah, 16-19, 25, 65.
Berman, Morris,5.
Bilqis, 95.

Caliph, Caliphate, 3, 6-9, 13, 20-1, 25, 29-30.
Centralization, 1, 4, 30, 39.
Chittick, William, 11, 33, 45, 47, 65.
Chodkiewicz, Michel, 19-20, 26, 37, 39, 48, 51, 65.
Corbin, Henry, 65.

Dahr, 93
Darqutni, 41.
Development, 2, 6, 16, 38.
Dhikr, 43, 49, 88, 94.
Din,vi, xi, 21, 36, 43-4.

Easton, David, 10.
Ellul, Jacques, 5.

Feyerabend, Paul, 5.
Foucault, vii, 5, 13, 25-6, 100, 103.
Fundamentalism, vii, x, 1, 3-4, 7-8, 12-13, 16, 18.

Ghazali, 7, 14, 18.

Habermas, vii.
Hadith, 10, 14, 17, 20-2, 30, 33, 40, 41-2, 47, 49, 52-4, 58-9, 62, 64, 66, 68-9, 71, 73, 83-4, 88-9, 91-3.
Hakim, x, 3, 36, 38, 48, 53.
Hakim, Besim Selim, 14.
Hal, 101.
Hallaq, Wael B., 28.
Haqqiqah, 66, 88.
Haraj, 54-5.
Haruri, 17.
Hawan, 41.
Hukm, ix-x, 17, 29, 31-4, 36-8, 42-4, 49, 52-4, 56, 60, 80-1, 98.
Hukumah, 3.

Ibahiyyah, 16, 18-19, 85.
Ibn Manzur, 3, 12, 16, 31-2, 40, 42, 46-7, 49-51, 54-5, 60, 69, 71, 74, 77, 84-5, 87-8, 90-1, 93-4, 97-8.
Ibn Taymiyyah, 3-4, 8, 12-13, 19.
Ibn Khaldun, 7.
Ibn Hajar, vi, vii, 19, 41, 69, 83.
Ibn Hanbal, 19, 53, 63.
Ijtihad, 28-31, 33-6, 41, 44-5, 47, 52-3, 80, 82.
Illich, Ivan, 5.
Ilm, 15.
Imamah, 7, 13, 23, 40.
Iman, 56, 63.
Imru al-Qays, 32, 46, 76-7, 84, 90.
Incarnation, 87.
Intercession, 56-8.
Islamic state, 3, 7, 12, 14.
Istighfar, 11.
Itibar, 26, 42, 49, 58.

Jahannam, 58-9.
Jarr, 71, 75-6.

Keller, Noah Ha Mim, 39, 48.
Khalifah, 13, 95.
Khass, 88, 96.
Khawarij, 16-19.
Khayr, 55, 59.
Khidr, 46.
Khuff, 31-2.
Khulafa, 95.
Khutbah, 69.
Kufr, 93-4, 97.

Lyons, Oren, 2, 12.

Machiavelli, 5.
Madhahib, 29.
Madhhab, 30, 54, 64.
Mander, Jerry, 2, 12-13.
Mantuq, 41, 44.
Manzoor, Parvez, 12, 14, 26.
Maskut, 41, 44.
Mawardi, 7-8.
Mayl, 87-8.
McGee, Travis, 5.
Meister Eckhardt, vii.
Morris, James Winston, 51, 65.
Mujahidah, 57.
Mujtahid, 28-9, 34, 47, 52-4.
Mumford, Lewis, 6.
Mumin, 56, 63.
Munajah, 43, 49.
Munif, Abdelrahman, 6, 13.
Murata, Sachiko, vii.
Mutazilahs, 7, 70,101.

Nafs, 41.
Nizam al-Mulk, 7.

Police, 5.
Polysemantism, 65-7, 80, 82.

Qada, 2, 28-9, 35-6, 41, 45.
Qadi, 2, 10, 28-9, 36-8, 44-5, 53, 82.
Qayyum, 93.
Qiyas, 34-5, 41-4, 47, 50, 53-4, 82.
Quaker, 39.
Quran, vii, viii, 1, 12, 14, 16, 18-24, 35, 39, 40, 42, 48-9, 51-2, 55, 65*ff*, 85-7, 97, 100.

Ray, 47, 53, 62, 82.
Rosen, Lawrence, 2, 4, 12-13, 36-7, 47.

Sabr, 16.
Said, Edward, 48, 99.

Sharani, 20, 29, 45, 48.
Shariah, vii, ix, 7, 9, 11-12, 15, 17, 20, 25, 29-34, 43, 52, 59, 61, 66, 90-1.
Shi'ism, viii, ix, 3, 7, 9, 13, 19, 69, 79, 85.
Shirk, 94.
Silsilah, 21.
Siyasah, 30-1.
State, 1-9, 11-12, 14, 20, 26, 28-31, 34-5, 38-9, 41, 82.
Sufi scholar, ix, 15, 31, 100.
Sufism, vii, ix, 3, 15-16, 18, 20, 25, 36, 46, 100-1.
Suicide, 57-8.
Sulh, 10.
Sultan, Sultanate, 3, 6, 9, 11, 28-31, 38, 41, 82.

Tafaqquh, vii, 9, 36, 43.
Tafriq / firq, 55.
Tafsil, 58.
Taharah, 6, 31, 33, 37, 42-4, 72, 79, 82-3.
Taqayyid, 82.
Taqiyah, 19.
Taqlid, 36, 42-3.
Tawil, 60, 65, 94.
Tayammum, 42-4, 72-3.
Thoreau, Henry, 8.

Ulema, ix, 1-4, 6, 11, 15-16, 19, 24-5, 29-31, 34-5, 38-41, 43, 46, 48, 51-3, 57, 79, 87-8.
Umara, 52.
Umm Waraqah, 41.
Ummal / amil, 51.
Unity of Existence, viii.
Usul al-fiqh, 13, 15.

Vogel, Frank, 28, 30, 35, 45.

Wahdat al-wujud, viii, 19.
Waliy, 94.
Waqiah, 57.
Waqt, 56.
Weiner, Norbert, 1, 12.
Wilaya, 52.
Wudu, 31, 35, 40, 43, 46, 55-6, 66*ff*, 79, 83, 85.

Zahir, 20, 32, 34, 39-40.
Zahiri, 70, 79, 85.